MARC PROULX

Hartford Moves

CORNELSEN
ENGLISH
LIBRARY

Cornelsen

CORNELSEN **ENGLISH** LIBRARY
Marc Proulx · Hartford Moves

Verlagsredaktion: Lena Posingies
Umschlaggestaltung: hawemannundmosch, Konzeption und Gestaltung, Berlin
Titelbild: Shutterstock.com/Alter-ego
Technische Umsetzung: Reemers Publishing Services GmbH

www.cornelsen.de

1. Auflage, 3. Druck 2025

Alle Drucke dieser Auflage sind inhaltlich unverändert
und können im Unterricht nebeneinander verwendet werden.

Druck: AZ Druck und Datentechnik GmbH, Kempten

ISBN 978-3-06-036257-8

PEFC-zertifiziert
Dieses Produkt
stammt aus
nachhaltig
bewirtschafteten
Wäldern und
kontrollierten Quellen
PEFC/04-31-2260   www.pefc.de

Contents

Chapter 1

"Cool it." That's what they tell you when you're so mad you could rip a tree out of the ground. Cool it. How dumb is that? Like you can just flip a switch and *bam* – the anger is gone. Those people have no idea.

5 I mean people like Mrs. Gonzalez. She's the one who had brought me to the main office. She's my PE teacher, one of those adults who seem to have forgotten what it's like to be a teenager. People like her either have very short memories or just don't want to remember.

10 It's not easy to sit quietly on a hard wooden bench when you're steaming like I was, especially when people are calmly walking in and out, acting like everything is perfectly fine. They obviously didn't know what had happened and why I was there. Mrs. Gupta, the school secretary, knew why I was 15 there, though. She looked over and smiled, like she felt sorry for me.

"Mr. Barnes will be with you in a moment, Iris. He's just getting your file," she said.

Great, I thought. *Do I look like I want to speak to the school* 20 *principal?*

The office door swung open and Mr. Barnes walked in. He was all business in his suit and tie. Mrs. Gupta looked happy to see him. I couldn't share the feeling. Mr. Barnes nodded to her, then looked over at me and sighed. He was holding a 25 folder in his hand and I could see my name on it. He marched towards his office door.

"This way, Miss Quinn," he said.

Inside his office, he pointed with the folder to the chair opposite his desk and waited for me to take a seat. Then he dropped the folder on the desk with a "plop" and sat down.

"So what's your version of the story, Miss Quinn? I've just heard Miss Mitchell's version and Mrs. Gonzalez's version," he said.

I had to think about that for a second. Angel had already told her story before me. That didn't seem fair.

"It wasn't my fault," I blurted. It was maybe not the best start. Mr. Barnes didn't look very moved.

"Let's start at the beginning. What exactly happened in the cafeteria? ... In your view," he said.

I rolled my eyes and exhaled. "I came into the cafeteria, stood in line, which took forever as usual, grabbed a lunch tray, saw the menu and knew I was definitely getting the veggie burger and fries and not the boring chili con carne. I finally got my food and looked for a place to sit. As usual, everybody was in their silly little groups and nobody wanted me to sit with them," I said. Since I had the school principal's attention, I wanted him to know about my sucky situation at this sucky school. "So, as usual, I sat down at the first open spot I could find. It's not like I wanted to sit near Angel. I didn't even notice her at first. She was sitting across from me, looking at me like I was a bad smell," I said.

"According to Mrs. Gonzalez, you two had some differences in PE just before lunch," Mr. Barnes said.

We had some differences? I thought. *Why do teachers and principals always talk like that? How about we almost got in a fight?*

"That wasn't my fault either," I said. "Just because I stole the ball from Angel in basketball, she got all hot and bothered."

The scene in PE was fresh in my mind. We were in a full-court, five-on-five game and Mrs. Gonzalez was the referee. I was having a great game. I should explain that I love basketball, and if I were taller (like a lot taller) I'd probably be on the girl's basketball team. Okay, I need to work on my ball-handling skills a bit, but I can shoot, and that day I was hotter than a pistol. Unfortunately, Angel Mitchell was too, and she was on the other team. She's about a foot taller and thinks she can do what she wants. I mean, yeah, she gets almost every rebound and has a pretty sweet jump shot (maybe a little better than mine but not much, I swear), but I was sure we had the better team. When you're my size, you have to be quick. You pass and run around a lot, bother your opponent and try to steal the ball. Yelling helps too. That's my game. Angel says I'm annoying, and if your opponent says that, then you're probably doing something right. Right?

"Mrs. Gonzalez says you fouled Angel several times," Mr. Barnes said. "Is that true?"

That was *so* not true – at least not from my perspective.

"Maybe I fouled her once. It was a rough game," I said.

"Apparently you pushed her hard after she blocked two of your shots," he said.

Geez, I thought. *Mrs. Gonzalez has an eye for detail.*

"That I don't remember," I said, which was true.

"Your PE teacher obviously remembers," he said.

This little info-war wasn't going well. I started getting steamed up again. My ears were warm and my right leg wouldn't stop bouncing up and down. Mr. Barnes looked at me and raised his hands from the desk.

"Take it easy, Miss Quinn. This is not a police interrogation," he said.

"It sure feels like one," I mumbled. 5

He sighed. "Let's get back to what happened in the cafeteria."

My mind went straight back to the scene ...

Angel:	*Do you have to sit here?*
Me:	*Does this table belong to you? I don't see your name on* 10 *it.*
Angel:	*If you eat the way you play, I don't want you near me.*
Me:	*If you can't handle the way I play, you probably can't handle much of anything.*
	(I know, it's a dumb thing to say, but, hey, when you're 15 provoked ...)
Angel:	*I can't? I think I handled it pretty well. Look who won the game? (smiling)*
Me:	*(explosion)*

Mr. Barnes interrupted my thoughts. "If you're having trou- 20 ble remembering, let me help you. Mrs. Gonzalez says she saw you stand up and empty the contents of your lunch tray all over Angel."

That was a colorful description. Mrs. Gonzalez didn't miss anything when she was on cafeteria duty. 25

"Now, why did you do that, Miss Quinn?" he asked.

"She said some nasty things," I said.

"You could have gotten up and walked away. You could have told Mrs. Gonzalez," he pointed out.

Neither seemed like an option to me at the time.

"I did get up! But I picked up my tray a little too fast," I said. His eyebrow shot up. I wasn't getting anywhere with this guy.

5 "Let me be clear," he said, tapping one of his long fingers against the desktop. "We don't tolerate that kind of behavior in this school."

I crossed my arms and sunk down in my chair. "I think I got that," I said.

10 Mr. Barnes sighed again, put some funky-looking reading glasses on, and opened the folder with my name on it. I leaned forward and tried to see what was in there. He glared at me, so I sat back again.

"Iris Quinn, 14 years old, born in Oakland, California, 15 moved to Weed, California. Attended Weed Elementary School, then Weed Middle School." He nodded quietly. I think he didn't get many kids like me.

"I see this is your first year at South End. You've only been here about two months," he said.

20 I knew what he was going to say next.

"It looks like you've already managed to get the attention of several of your teachers," he said.

"I guess they like me," I said.

His eyebrow shot up again. "Their comments here don't 25 exactly confirm that," he said.

He wasn't finished. There was a lot in that file.

"You don't seem to have any brothers or sisters at this school," he said. "Do you have any siblings at all?"

No one had asked me that before, at least not in the last 30 two years. I thought for a moment, then shook my head.

"Was that a 'no', or are you not sure?" he asked.

He had no idea how close to the truth he was. Does your brother ever really stop being your brother? I didn't say anything.

He closed the file, took off his funky-looking glasses, leaned back in his squeaky chair and rubbed his eyes. 5

"Miss Quinn, it's not my business why you and your family moved here to Hartford," he said. "But I do understand that it's a big change to move across the country to a new place and a new school. It's probably been very stressful for you."

I hadn't really looked at our move that way. But I wasn't 10 going to argue with him just when he was showing some sympathy.

I suddenly thought: *This might turn out okay after all ...*

Then he continued, "But that doesn't excuse your behavior." 15

... or maybe not, I thought.

"At this school we have a three-strikes-and-you're-out policy," he said.

"Three strikes and you're out? Like in baseball?"

"Exactly. Like in baseball," he said in a serious tone. 20

Baseball isn't really my game, but I know that when the pitcher throws the ball and you swing the bat and miss, it's a strike. And if you get three of those, you're out. Your turn to hit the ball is over. I know because I've gotten a lot of strikes. I also know that people use baseball expressions way too 25 much.

"You have one strike, Miss Quinn," Mr. Barnes said, pulling me out of my thoughts. I understood right away.

"What? No way! What about Angel?" I protested.

"Never mind about Miss Mitchell," he said. "You've got 30 two more chances, young lady."

"And if I get three strikes?" I knew what was coming.

"Then you're out. Suspended. You can't come back to school for two weeks," he answered.

He didn't wait for my reaction. He closed my file, dropped
5 it in his desk drawer and slammed the drawer shut.

"That'll be all for today, Miss Quinn," he said.

I hate baseball.

Chapter 2

The last bell of the day rang and I didn't waste any time. I shoved my notebook in my backpack and didn't even say goodbye to Mr. Wentworth, my English teacher. After PE and the events at lunchtime, I hadn't spoken to anybody for the rest of the day. I knew that kids were looking at me and talking about me. "Look, there's Iris the troublemaker. The big-mouthed kid from California."

When I sat down in the school bus, I realized I wasn't in a big hurry to get home. The last thing Mr. Barnes had told me before I stomped out of his office was that my parents would be informed. *Fantastic,* I thought.

As the bus rolled along South Street, I stared out the window at the cars and bikes and clapboard houses. Hartford doesn't look too bad from a school bus window, like the state capitol with its huge shiny dome, and the nicer neighborhoods with their big houses with big porches and probably a zillion rooms. That's not our part of town, though. South End, where we live, is a lot less glamorous. The houses are smaller and close together, and a lot of them don't even have front yards. That doesn't bother me. Our neighborhood in Weed wasn't much different. What bothers me is that it's not home. It feels like a foreign country – or what I imagine a foreign country to feel like. In Weed everything was familiar. It felt like mine. Here I don't feel anything. That sucks.

The brakes screeched and the bus stopped at the corner of Franklin and Vine. That's my stop. Chance, our chatty bus driver, threw open the doors.

"There you go, campers! Get home safe," he said.

5 Vine Street is pretty unspectacular. In fact, streets don't get more boring than this one. I was complaining to myself as I walked along, then a loud noise made me turn around. An ambulance and a police car raced past on Franklin. The screaming sirens and flashing blue and red lights made my
10 head swim ...

The smell of pine trees is thick in the dry afternoon air. I'm dragging the big plastic bag full of grass and weeds down the driveway to the trash cans by the side of the road. Dad is in the back yard where I left him, and Mom and Matty are in the house. I
15 *hear little kids' voices down the road. They're screaming and calling out, probably playing streetball or something. I should tell Matty to hop on his bike and we'll check it out. The little guy never likes to miss the fun, and I like to make sure he doesn't.*

I hear sirens. They're getting louder and louder. A para-
20 *medic rescue truck and a fire truck suddenly turn the corner and zip past the house. Wow, I think. How often does that happen? Mom's voice cuts through the noise.*

"Iris, where's Matty? Is he out there with you?" she says from a window.

25 *"I thought he was with you," I say.*

"No, I told you to–"

I don't hear the rest because I'm looking down the road. The red trucks have stopped and doors are opening. Everything is dancing in blue and red light.

It's like I'm running before I even know I'm running. I feel my heart pumping.

As I get nearer, I see kids and grown-ups standing around. I hear the crackle of a two-way radio. Beyond the trucks, a car is stopped in the middle of the road. I see our neighbor Mrs. 5 *Martin with her hand over her mouth. I push past her. Beyond a parked car, between the legs of firefighters and paramedics, I see a bike in the road. The front wheel is a broken tangle of metal and rubber. The bike frame is blue with orange stripes. Just like the one that stood in our living room by the Christmas* 10 *tree, all shiny and new with a big red ribbon on it. ...*

The tears felt cold on my face. So many tears ... But I wasn't crying. Huh? I looked around and saw cold water spraying out from between the plants in someone's garden. The gentle spray was dotting my face and clothes. I realized I was in 15 front of Mrs. Gibson's house. Her faded white wooden fence barely contained the thick tangle of trees and bushes and flowers.

"Hey!" I protested. The water stopped.

"Hey back," a raspy old voice said. "Is that you, Erin 20 Quinn?"

"Iris!" I said loudly

"Iris," she said. "Ain't that what I said?"

"You got me wet!" I said, looking at the water spots on my faded jean jacket and black Foo Fighters T-shirt. 25

"Well, why are you standing there, girl?" she answered.

I moved a few steps along the sidewalk to get a clear view of her. She stood in a flowery summer dress and a buttoned-up red cardigan sweater. She was holding a garden hose and I noticed for the first time how the knobby knuck- 30 les on her hands looked like dark old oak trees. The afternoon sun was making the deep wrinkles on her brown face look even deeper.

"I wasn't standing, I was walking," I said, annoyed.

5 "Well, maybe next time you need to walk faster!" she said, chuckling.

Mrs. Gibson was one of the first people besides Chance the bus driver who I'd met here. She was probably the only neighbor I ever saw, and definitely the only one who kept 10 a garden. She had a big hammer of a voice for an old black lady who wasn't much taller than me. Sometimes I'd hear her from a distance, talking and laughing, but nobody was there with her, and I'm pretty sure she wasn't talking on a cell phone. The neighbors probably thought she was crazy. 15 Maybe she was.

"Are you just gonna stand there or are you gonna make yourself useful?" she said, bending over and pulling a weed out of the ground.

I wasn't really interested in chatting, or in helping an old 20 lady in her garden. At the same time, going home to face the Inquisition was even less attractive.

"Whatever," I sighed, pushing open the garden gate.

"You take that," she said, handing me the garden hose straight away. I let my backpack drop to the ground. "Just 25 don't water those too much, they're special," she said, pointing to some small flowers with tiny blue and white petals. Then she shuffled off towards her little house, leaving me to do her work. *Great,* I thought.

I'd never seen a garden like this. There was nothing neat 30 and tidy about it. It looked like she'd plopped things down and planted them without much thought. In between all the plants and flowers there was other stuff – piles of rounded stones, pieces of colored glass, driftwood. There were also wind-chimes hanging from branches and weird toy figures and ceramic animals and a rusty old car license plate from the state of Georgia. 5

"Watch what you're doin' now." I jumped as her loud voice cut through the silence.

"Geez, you scared me," I said.

"You can't just water in one place. They all gotta get some. Like this," she said, snatching the hose out of my hand and 10 swinging it back and forth. The water flew all around and I had to step back. As quickly as she'd started, she dropped the hose. She looked at me and pointed to something over my shoulder.

"Drink your lemonade before the ice melts," she said. 15

She shuffled over to an old wooden table where two tall glasses of iced lemonade were standing. The water was still flowing out of the hose.

"Erm, Mrs. Gibson?" I said, pointing to the hose.

"Turn that off, would you please?" she said. "And you can 20 call me Mae, like everybody else does."

The lemonade was fresh, super sweet and cold, just how I like it. *This lady can't be too crazy*, I thought. *Or maybe crazy people make the best lemonade.*

"I've never seen nobody drink my lemonade and still have 25 a face as long as yours," she said. "What on earth is troubling you, child?"

I couldn't ignore her question. I sighed and told her about PE, about what had happened in the cafeteria, about my meeting with the principal, and about how my parents were probably waiting at home to talk to me about it all.

She listened, rolling the ice around in her glass. Then she shook her head and clicked her tongue. "My goodness. What did you say her name was?"

"Angel. Angel Mitchell," I said. The name left a bad taste in my mouth.

"How are you two gonna sort that out?" she said. "You can't just ignore each other for the whole school year."

She was right. The idea didn't make me feel any better. I didn't say anything.

"Weed," she said after a long pause.

"Huh?" I said.

"You must get a lot of jokes about that name," she said. I had told her about our big move when we had last talked.

"But it ain't the strangest or funniest name for a place, I can tell you," she said. "Have you ever heard of Whynot, North Carolina? Or Ninety-six? That's in South Carolina. I've been to 'em both. Between, Georgia too."

"Are you kidding me?" I said.

Her face brightened. "I knew I could make you smile," she said. "They weren't very nice places back then. Weed's probably nicer."

She finished her lemonade, then slapped her hand down on the table. I jumped again.

"Do you know what those are?" she said, pointing at some tall, purple flowers in a clump of green. I shrugged.

"Irises. And the stuff around them? Weeds." She looked at me. "A good place for you to start," she said. "Use that." She pointed to a tool with a long handle and something on the end that looked like a bird's foot.

"Huh? What for?" I said.

"To get those weeds out of there so that those Irises can shine," she said. "Or are you in a hurry to get home?"

She knew the answer. I sighed.

"Can I at least finish my lemonade?" 5

She patted my hand. "You'll be just fine, Iris Quinn."

Man, if only I could believe it, I thought.

Chapter 3

Vine Street feels even more depressing when the daylight is gone. Maybe it's the boring shoebox-like houses with their lifeless front yards. Or maybe the happy American flags that our no-name neighbors hang in front of their boring houses,
5 like every day is one big Fourth of July.

Our own little shoebox with its peeling blue paint was squeezed in neatly between the other shoeboxes. I walked in the front door, dropped my backpack and went to hang up my jean jacket on the coat hooks next to the door. The whole
10 wall was vibrating like a giant electric toothbrush. *Weird,* I thought. A rumbling noise from the other side of the wall was getting louder. The rumble then turned into a moan, then a shriek, like a sick bird.

"What the–?" I said.

15 A small crack appeared next to the coat hooks and another one crossed it. Something was growing out of the wall, like one of those freaky horror-movie scenes. Dust and bits of green paint were falling onto the wood floor. Then a spinning drill popped out of the wall. It stopped and every-
20 thing was silent. The drill disappeared back into the wall, leaving a good-sized hole that I could see through. I saw a blinking eye at the other end of the hole and heard Dad's voice.

"Oh man. Did that just happen?" he said.

25 "I'd say yes," I answered.

I walked around to the living room, where he was standing with the power drill in one hand and white dust in his beard. He looked at me.

"Let me guess. You didn't mean to do that," I said.

"Let's not mention it to Mom," he said. 5

"Oh, sure," I said. "Like a hole in the wall is the most normal thing in the world."

Dad's eyes searched around.

"A picture would go well there," he said.

Dad still hadn't found a job. With way too much time 10 on his hands, he'd decided that fixing up the place himself was a better idea than paying someone to do it. Mom and I weren't so sure. Every new home improvement project was like a home disaster waiting to happen. This time, at least, the hole in the wall was a welcome distraction. I left him to 15 plot his next move and disappeared upstairs to my room.

Some people say you can get used to anything. Well, I still haven't gotten used to seeing two bedrooms instead of three at the top of those creaky stairs. Matty's toys scattered over the carpet, his wild drawings taped to the walls of his room, 20 his stuffed animals waiting patiently for him on his messy bed – it's all missing. I don't think Mom and Dad thought about what it would mean to have one less bedroom. Mom wanted to buy this house, so I blame it on her. What was she thinking? The big empty hole in the middle of everything, like 25 the hole in that wall downstairs, wasn't getting any smaller.

I was staring at the unpacked boxes in the corner of my room when Dad called me for dinner an hour later. On the kitchen table was a steaming dish of lasagna. It smelled amazing. Fun fact: Dad's way better at cooking than he is 30 at building and fixing things. Matty and I used to help him in the kitchen. Dad told us what we needed, we fetched the ingredients, then he showed us how it all goes together. We made everything from tacos to tuna casserole. But all that feels like a past life now. Probably because it is.

"Could you pass the salad, Iris?" Mom said.

She had come home from work, tossed her jacket and shoulder bag on the antique chair in the hallway and walked straight past the new wall feature. Dad hadn't said a word about it. When I sat down at the table, he gave me one of his we-know-something-she-doesn't-know-and-let's-keep-it-that-way looks across the table.

"Mm. This lasagna is actually tasty!" Mom said, acting surprised.

Dad nodded. "Of course it is."

It was a joke in the family. Mom with her Italian roots loved to tease Dad with his Irish background whenever he cooked Italian food.

"What happened at school today, Iris?" Mom asked.

My heart jumped and I nearly dropped my fork. "Just let me explain," I blurted out.

Mom stopped chewing and looked at me, her eyebrows raised. She looked at Dad. She clearly didn't know what I was talking about, and now I had just let the cat out of the bag. But Dad knew – I could see it in his face.

"Why don't you tell us about it, Iris?" he said finally.

"About what?" Mom said, still surprised.

Dad looked at me. I hadn't thought about how I would sell this situation to them. I had to think fast.

"I don't know what it is about that school," I said, choosing to start slowly.

Dad was more direct. "Mr. Barnes mentioned an incident in the cafeteria," he said.

"Mr. Barnes?" Mom's alarm bells started ringing. "Isn't he the principal? You spoke with the *principal*?"

"He called this afternoon," Dad replied.   5

Mom looked hard at me across the table. My appetite was disappearing.

"I'm waiting, Iris," she said.

"Look, it wasn't my fault," I said finally.

"What exactly wasn't your fault?" she asked.   10

When I didn't answer, Dad gave it a try.

"What did you have for lunch today, Iris?" he asked.

I had to play his game. "A veggie burger and fries."

"And how did it taste?" he continued, looking at me with a sly smile. I rolled my eyes.   15

"I don't know, okay?" I said.

Mom was looking back and forth at us both, trying to put the puzzle pieces together.

"Because …" she said slowly, waiting for me to complete the sentence. Dad jumped in.   20

"Let's just say that Iris's cafeteria lunch landed somewhere else besides in her mouth," he said.

Dad always has a colorful way with words. I think it's an Irish thing. Mom put her fork and knife down.

"Okay, I don't need to hear the rest," she said. "This is the   25
third time you've been in trouble this school year, Iris."

"Mr. Barnes called it 'strike one,'" Dad said. "You're not batting very well this season, Iris."

"Oh, please, no baseball talk!" I said. "Look. I'm sorry."

It was time to show some regret. Well, at least a little.   30

"It wouldn't have happened if Angel Mitchell hadn't been so pig-headed and ... and ... lippy."

"Lippy?" Dad said. "Well, you should know all about being lippy."

5 I glared at him. "What do you mean by that?"

"Iris, it's been one thing after another since we moved here," Mom said. "What is going on?"

Mr. Barnes hardly knew me, but he understood me better than my own parents. My ears were getting warm.

10 "Maybe it hasn't been so easy for me. Okay? Did you ever think of that?" I said. "Hartford is a long way from Weed. And South End is a crappy school." Hearing the emotion in my voice, they looked at each other.

"We've talked about this, Iris. We understand that it's dif-
15 ficult," Mom said quietly. "But we really think this move is for the best. Right, honey?" She looked at Dad. He didn't answer. She leaned forward. "Alex."

"I guess we'll see," he said finally. Mom didn't look very satisfied with that answer.

20 "Ha! You see?" I said. "How do you know it's for the best? So far, it's been pretty sucky, if you ask me."

"You know I don't like that word," Mom said.

"Which word? Sucky? What's wrong with it? Everybody uses it," I said.

25 "It's an ugly word. The point is that we need this, Iris. We need a way to ... to move on ... to restart," Mom said.

"Why can't we move on without leaving everything behind?" I asked. Dad looked at Mom like the same question was on his mind. We'd had this conversation before, but this
30 time Dad seemed to be on my side.

Mom's lips tightened. "Guys, we decided in Weed that we needed to change something. You told me, Alex, how stuck you felt. We were all stuck," she said. Dad looked at his plate. "Hartford is giving us a chance to move forward. It's a good place for us now," she said.

"That's easy for you to say, Mom. You're from here," I said, poking at my salad. She was looking at me. I knew I was right and I knew she knew I was right.

"We wouldn't have come if I hadn't got this job. You know that. It's not just about me coming back," she said.

"Iris is right," Dad said, breaking his silence. "You have your old contacts – your brother, your family friends. You wouldn't have gotten that job without Vinnie's help, and that's okay. But what about me? Anywhere else, companies would be looking for IT professionals. I mean, are these people living in the Stone Age?"

I've never understood exactly what Dad does. Something with businesses and computer systems. He tried to explain it once and it sounded pretty boring. It's easier to understand what a librarian does. Mom used to bring home books all the time that she thought Matty and I would like. She didn't always get it right, but if her grand plan was to make us read more, it worked.

"I know you're frustrated, honey," she said, reaching for Dad's hand. He held onto his fork and pushed the lasagna around his plate. "At least my family connections can help us," she continued. "You know, working in the county courthouse isn't my dream job. I miss the libraries. I miss that work." She sighed. "And I miss what we had as much as you guys do."

Things got quiet. A lot of our dinners went this way. It was Mom who always tried to change the mood. She sat up.

"I suggested to Dad that a little barbecue this Saturday would be nice. We haven't had one here yet and we won't
5 have many more chances before it gets colder," she said.

Fine. Whatever, I thought.

"We'll get chicken for you. Uncle Vinnie and Aunt Gwen said they'll bring steaks and potato salad," she said.

When I heard the last part, I rolled my eyes. "Didn't we
10 just see Uncle Vinnie last weekend?" I could deal with Aunt Gwen, but Uncle Vinnie was hard work.

"Oh, come on, Iris," Mom said.

Dad was going along with Mom's idea. He looked at me. "What do you say?"

15 I sighed and got dramatic. "What choice do I have? I wouldn't want to be the party pooper, would I?"

They looked at each other.

"Well, you're already one," Dad said.

I grabbed my plate, slid back my chair and got up.

20 "I'm not hungry anymore," I announced.

"Wonderful. Be that way," Dad said. "Don't forget to put your plate in the dishwasher." He shoved a forkful of lasagna in his mouth.

I decided he wasn't going to have the last word.

25 "By the way, how's that hole in the wall?" I said.

He stopped chewing and stared at his plate. A thin piece of mozzarella hung from his beard. Mom looked up at me, then at Dad.

"Hole in the wall?"

Chapter 4

"Let's not waste time, people. You gentlemen at the back, could you please stop talking and find a partner?"

That was Mrs. Jameson. It was time for partner work again and I wasn't thrilled. Don't get me wrong. Social Studies is actually one of my better classes. Not all the stuff we 5 do is totally boring. At the moment we were doing the civil rights movement. It's a topic that seemed to have most of the class sitting up in their seats, including me. It's history, but it's still going on, if you know what I mean.

I knew most of the kids in class by now, at least by name. 10 One of them, sadly, was Angel Mitchell. This was the only other class we had together besides PE. In the first week, I thought maybe she was someone I could connect with. That idea went out the window after things got heated in PE the first time. By the second week we were sitting as far away 15 from each other as possible.

Jason Lee was also in our class. His family runs the Korean grocery store over on Franklin Avenue. Once he helped me find some spices that Dad sent me there to get. He's smart in class and, the way he moves, I can see he's probably good 20 at sports. If I had to partner with him, I wouldn't mind it too much.

He was sitting behind Kellyann Moore, who stands out in class like a white YouTube goddess. Perfect posture, immaculate skin, neat hair, carefully chosen clothes. Next to her I felt 25 like a slob. But there's something else about her. She has an attitude and an opinion about everything. A bit like me, actually, but better-looking. Maybe that's why I felt small around her. She has her devoted followers – Faith Jenkins and a guy named J.J. Hannigan, who sits with his legs spread wide and acts like he owns the school. I'm just going to say it. He's a jerk. The three of them were constantly whispering, giggling and passing little notes between them, making everyone else feel like they weren't invited to the party. Weird.

"Iris, who's your partner?" Mrs. Jameson said. Before I could answer, she added, "Lalo, you don't have a partner. Why don't you two work together?"

Lalo Mendez was sitting behind me. He's one of those kids who you forget is in the classroom because he's so quiet. I think he likes it that way, maybe because he's so big, and I don't mean just tall.

"Yeah, sure," he said.

When I turned and looked up at him, he leaned back in his seat, like he thought I was going to slap him or something.

"I mean ... if you want to," he said.

I had thought Lalo was one of those Latino boys trying to be tough and cool in his black sweatpants, high-top sneakers and oversized, button-down shirt. Looking at him now, there was nothing tough about him. His face was soft and round. He didn't smile a lot, but he seemed to want to.

I remembered the scene the week before when Kellyann, Faith and J.J. were giggling just before class started. Kellyann reacted to something J.J. said.

"Who? *Him?*" she said, pointing at Lalo sitting in the next row.

She looked at him like he was a piece of rotten fruit, then snorted, pretending to hide her laughter. Most of the class saw it. I think he pretended not to notice it. He knew the kids around him were looking at him.

"Okay, Iris?" Mrs. Jameson said. 5

"Fine, whatever," I said. I slowly turned my desk around to face his.

We got further than I thought we would. Mrs. Jameson showed us a timeline in our textbook with major events of the civil rights era. We had to pick an event and report on it. 10 I was being pushy, as usual. Lalo suggested Brown vs. Board of Education. That's the Supreme Court decision that said you can't put blacks and whites in separate public schools. I shot down that idea pretty fast. Any topic that had to do with school turned me off. And court decisions didn't excite 15 me either. When I said that, Lalo stayed quiet and didn't look up. He played with the pen in his hand. I looked again at the choices.

"Let's do the Freedom Rides," I said.

I wasn't sure what it was all about, but it sounded like 20 some kind of road trip, which was interesting enough. And "freedom" is one of those words with a bell attached to it, as Mom likes to say.

Lalo thought about it, then shrugged. "Sure," he said.

That was too easy, I thought. I was expecting more push- 25 back from the big guy. Now we had to start working, which I'd wanted to avoid for as long as possible. I gave him a disappointed look, slid back in my chair and pulled the textbook towards me.

"Fine. Let's get going, then," I said. "I'll read out the interesting stuff and you make notes."

Lalo sat still. He looked up and studied me for a moment. I noticed a tiny earring hidden in the flesh of one of his ears. A little smile grew across his big face.

"How about we take turns?" he said.

Normally I'd argue, but for some reason I didn't. Maybe because I was dealing with a very big dude. Or maybe it was something else about him.

"Okay, but you write first," I said.

After school, the bus was filling up fast. I squeezed past two chatty girls standing in the aisle and sat down in the seat in front of them. One of them looked annoyed.

"Dang, girl! Are you in a hurry or what?" she said.

"It's a bus, guys, not a shopping mall," I said.

They looked at each other and rolled their eyes. A big figure appeared behind them. It was Lalo. I was confused. Lalo Mendez on this bus? He wasn't surprised to see me.

"Hey," he said softly.

"Hey yourself," I said. "Are you new on this bus?"

"Nah. I usually sit back there," he said, pointing with his chin to the back of the bus.

I realized I hardly ever looked at the kids sitting at the back. Two boys were waiting behind Lalo.

"Come on, man! Move your big butt, Lalo!" they said.

"Oh well, see ya," he said, moving on.

"Adios," I said.

At Franklin and Vine the bus squealed to a stop and Chance opened the doors with his usual fanfare.

"*Carpe diem*, you people! Make the most of this lovely day!" he said. "Or what's left of it!" he laughed.

"Yes, Master Yoda," I said, climbing off the bus. As I walked away, I heard Chance again.

"Señor Mendez, have a good one, sir," he said. 5

I turned and there was Lalo with his backpack stepping off the bus. He looked at me.

"It's not my stop, but I can walk this way," he said.

We practically lived in the same neighborhood. For the first time I was walking down Vine with another kid from 10 school. It felt awkward. I didn't really want to talk about Social Studies. Luckily, Lalo didn't either.

"I saw what happened between you and Angel in the cafeteria," Lalo said.

What could I say? Hope you liked the show? 15

"I'd watch out for her, if I were you," he said. "Not just because she's bigger."

"I'm not scared of Angel," I said.

"I'm just saying," he said. "I've known Angel since third grade. She's got a hard head. A strong will. She's also got 20 issues," he said.

"Issues? What do you mean?" I said.

"Family stuff. I don't know the whole story. But I think it's pretty heavy," he said.

I thought about it and shook my head. If this guy only 25 knew who he was talking to.

"I guess we all have a story," I said.

Lalo was quiet. Then he said, "You haven't lived around here long, have you?"

"It feels like ages to me," I said. I wasn't sure if he got my humor until he smiled gently. He seemed curious about me. I wondered how much I could trust this guy.

"Where'd you live before?" he said.

5 "Northern California. A small town. You wouldn't know it," I said.

"What do you think of Hartford?" he asked.

Why not be honest, I thought. "It kind of sucks," I said.

"I know what you mean," he said. "My mom's from Puerto 10 Rico. I wish we were living there. It's way nicer."

"Puerto Rico." I rolled the words around in my mouth. What did I know about Puerto Rico? Zero. Well, not quite.

"Like Maria," I said.

Lalo looked at me. "Maria from *West Side Story*?"

15 I'd seen the musical on TV with Mom and Dad. Tough gang members in New York City, dancing and singing. Puerto Rican girls singing "I like to leeve een Amereeca". A Puerto Rican, Maria, falls in love with a white gang member, Tony. It was too much romance for me.

20 "Anita is actually more like my mom," he said.

I recalled Maria's friend. Strong accent, loud, pushy.

"Those are some badass high-tops," he said, changing the subject. He was pointing to my high-top Chucks, the only sneakers I ever wore. "What's up with the crazy colors?" My 25 left sneaker was covered in bright graffiti.

"Long story. It started with my little brother. Now my dad does it," I said. I didn't want to get into it.

"My mom buys me crazy-colored underwear," he said. "She says no one has to know. But everybody in PE knows," 30 he said.

Okay, this is embarrassing, I thought. *Do I want to know about his underwear?* I steered the subject back.

"I caught my brother, Matty, doodling on my shoe with coloring pens," I said. "I got really mad. But then I got over it. It's hard to stay mad at a Down kid." 5

Lalo looked at me. "Down syndrome? Oh yeah."

Lalo was clearly not a dummy. He'd understood and shown some feeling. Suddenly I didn't mind sharing.

"After that, Matty did his magic on every new pair of Chucks that I got," I said. 10

Lalo smiled. "Always the left shoe?"

I looked down at my Chucks. "Yep," I said.

"Beautiful," he said. "I like that."

He was honestly moved.

"So your dad does it now," he said. "Why not Matty?" 15

I wished I hadn't said it. We walked on.

"What about you? Any brothers or sisters?" I said, ignoring his question.

"Huh? Oh. A sister," he said. "She's older. She doesn't live with us. It's just me and my mom," he said. 20

I wondered if I should ask about his dad. We got to the corner of Bentley and Vine and stopped.

"I live down that way," he said, pointing down Bentley Avenue. It looked just as boring as Vine Street.

Something about Lalo didn't add up for me. Just like in 25 class, the big guy didn't fit the picture I had had of him. But the new picture was like a puzzle with one or two pieces missing.

The distant sound of a siren grew louder. A block away on Franklin, a police car screamed past with its lights flashing. 30

Lalo's face turned serious, like he'd seen an old enemy. He looked back at me. Then I had a thought.

"Which one's your favorite?" I asked.

Lalo looked surprised.

5 "You know, the characters in *West Side Story*," I said.

A little smile spread across his face.

"Maria," he said, looking at me.

I nodded, not even sure why I asked. Maybe it was those missing puzzle pieces. His answer didn't seem to help

10 though.

"See you at school," I said, and turned to cross Bentley.

Chapter 5

Mae's garden isn't the only place where the sun shines, but it sure seemed like it when I walked by her house. Behind the garden fence, a small figure that could only be Mae was moving around among the thick plants and bushes. I heard her big voice. ⁵

"It's God's weather, and he sure must be in a good mood today," she said without looking up. "Ain't that the truth, Iris Quinn?"

Mae was the only person I knew who called me by my first *and* last name. ¹⁰

I stood on the opposite side of the fence. "It's a good day if you have a garden," I said. Mae straightened her back slowly and looked at me through the branches.

"It's a good day anyway," she said. She sounded so sure I almost believed her. "Are you and that girl Angel still at it? I ¹⁵ can see something's on your mind again."

"Aw, do you have to bring that up?" I complained. I'd managed to forget about it after Lalo's comments. I tried to change the subject.

"Did you just hear that police car?" I said. ²⁰

"Yep. They're late for their coffee and donuts," she said with a chuckle.

"Do you like living here? I mean in Hartford?" I asked. I was still trying to understand the empty feeling this place gave me. Mae must have sensed it. ²⁵

"Give it time," she said. "There's good and bad wherever you go. It ain't no worse here than anyplace else – and it's a whole lot better than some places, I can tell you."

This is the way old people talk, I thought.

⁵ "Come in here for a second," she said.

"You won't put me to work again, will you?" I said.

She laughed. "I want to show you something," she insisted in a high voice. "Come on in here."

I opened the gate and pushed past the branches. I won't ¹⁰ lie – it felt nice in the coolness of all those plants with the warm sun peeking through. I could see why she spent so much time there. It was like a freaking oasis.

"Look at that," she said. She was pointing at the bed of flowers – the Irises that I'd worked on.

¹⁵ "No more weeds and look at them, standing all tall like they own the place. Ain't that beautiful?" she said.

She had a point. I shrugged. "I hope so, after all that work," I said.

She laughed. "Stop moaning, now. That wasn't nothin'. ²⁰ I'm not done with you yet, Iris Quinn."

Can't she just call me Iris? I thought.

"No garden work today, Mae, please," I said.

She waved her hand at me, like I was an annoying insect.

"Listen, I don't know what's bothering you about this ²⁵ place," she said. "We've got all different kinds of folks, and most of them are good people. Now, that's not to say bad things don't happen." She kicked aside some fallen leaves. "There's crime in South End like anywhere else. I watch the evening news. But I gotta say, sometimes those police cause ³⁰ more problems than they solve," she said.

"What do you mean?" I said.

"Never mind," she said. "I have nothing against officers of the law, as long as they're doing their job."

Why wouldn't they do their job? I thought. *What else would they do*? She wasn't making any sense.

"I don't know why people can't just get along. It ain't that hard. And that includes you and Angel," she said.

I shrugged again. "I'll stay out of her hair if she stays out of mine," I said.

Mae looked at me, then at the ground. "All these leaves have to go into that compost pile over there. And then–"

That was the signal. "Gotta go, Mae!" I said, stepping back towards the garden gate. "I have homework."

It was true. The Social Studies presentation was on my mind. I had to finish my part by Friday. Mae stood with her hands on her hips, watching me slip back out the gate. I wasn't sure if she was annoyed or amused.

"My goodness. Your parents have their hands full with you, Iris Quinn. You're so ... prickly!" she said.

"Bye, Mae Gibson!" I called over my shoulder.

"And fresh too!" she yelled back.

The old portable TV was on when I walked into the kitchen. I could smell paint. There was newspaper on the floor around an old wooden cupboard that Mom and Dad had bought days before at a garage sale. Half the cupboard was now light green and I swear it looked like someone had puked on it. Dad was busy with a paint brush.

On TV a serious-looking news reporter with a microphone was standing on a city street corner. Next to him were the words "BLACK LIVES" in big letters.

"For the second straight day, large crowds here in Milwaukee are on the streets. We've seen shops looted, cars set on fire, and violent clashes between protesters and police. Police chief Alisha Taylor told us just hours ago that several
5 people have been injured including two police officers. At least ten people have been arrested," he said.

"What's going on?" I said.

Dad didn't look up. "Oh, I'm just giving this old cupboard a fresh face."

10 "I mean in Milwaukee," I said.

Dad turned to the TV. "Oh, that," he said. "You didn't hear about it at school? Another police shooting. This time it's a younger kid. He's in the hospital."

"Wow. How old is he?" I asked.

15 "Around your age. Fourteen, I think," he said.

"Geez, what did he do wrong?"

"It's not clear. Two officers stopped him on the street and he tried to run away," Dad said.

"So they *shot* him?!"

20 "I don't understand it either," Dad said, shaking his head. "He's African-American."

"So? What difference does that make?" I said.

"Well, a big difference, actually," he said, sighing.

I heard the front door close and Mom's voice. "I'm home,"
25 she called. Seconds later she floated into the kitchen. She looked at the TV.

"Oh, the riots. Terrible, isn't it? I was talking with Vinnie about it earlier."

My Uncle Vinnie is a cop. He's been one as long as I can
30 remember. The times when he and Aunt Gwen came to visit in Weed, he was just Uncle Vinnie on vacation – relaxed and

jokey. He always had a little magic trick ready for us. I could figure them out every time while Matty sat with his mouth hanging open, his big eyes fixed on the amazing Uncle Vinnie. Sometimes he told us stories about working on the streets of Hartford, catching shoplifters, breaking up fights, helping old people. He acted like being a cop was the most normal job in the world.

"So what's Vinnie think?" Dad said, dipping his brush into the can of green paint.

"He says it's tough being a cop. Sometimes you have to make quick, life-or-death decisions. He doesn't think it's racial," Mom said. "He says the boy probably did something really stupid, and that people don't see that or don't want to," Mom said. "I can understand his point."

Dad stopped painting. "Come on, Bianca. Things like this happen too often. How can it not be racial?"

"I'm not saying it never is," Mom said. "But why do people automatically scream 'Black Lives Matter'?"

It was a touchy subject with Mom. I think she felt it was an attack on her own brother.

"People are angry. They want it to stop," Dad said.

"But don't *all* lives matter?" she said.

Dad looked at her, surprised. "Where did you hear that? From your brother? That's what whites say who don't want to face the race problem. It's a racist red flag."

Mom looked embarrassed. "I'm sorry, I didn't mean it that way."

Dad shook his head and turned back to the cupboard. He and Mom suddenly seemed miles apart. It was time to change the subject.

"Who chose the green?" I asked.

Dad stopped again and looked at his work. "What's wrong with it?" He looked at Mom for support.

She tilted her head. "Is that the color we agreed on?"

"I thought it was," Dad said.

5 They stood silently looking at the puke-green cupboard. Maybe I had picked the wrong subject.

Conveniently, I remembered my homework again. I don't think they even heard me excuse myself and disappear up to my room.

Chapter 6

After the Big Incident in the cafeteria, people suggested that I should stay away from there, or at least wait until most students had finished their lunch. You can probably imagine what I thought of that.

"Aren't you scared?" one kid asked me. 5

There's a lot I don't understand in this weird world, but one thing I know: when your personal universe has been shaken up like mine, nothing much scares you anymore.

The lunch menu had hardly changed. What a surprise! The veggie burger was still there, along with the tasteless 10 chicken biryani and the boring spaghetti bolognese. *These people have no imagination,* I thought. I got in line.

After getting my food, I took my lunch tray and found an empty table. A few kids at nearby tables were checking me out. I looked straight back at them. *Yeah, Iris the Trouble-* 15 *maker is back,* I thought. *Big deal. Get used to it.*

I opened my chocolate milk and took a big gulp. After a few bites of biryani, a girl's voice that I didn't recognize said, "Hey, look who it is." A moment later the same voice said, "Do you mind if we join you?" 20

Looking up, I was surprised and a bit confused to see Kellyann Moore with her two sidekicks, Faith and J.J., standing with their lunch trays, looking like lost sheep. Kellyann didn't wait for my answer. She sat down and the other two followed. It was awkward, to say the least. 25

"Hey, you got the biryani too!" Kellyann said, like we were now instant soulmates.

"Me too!" Faith said.

"Bolognese is the best," J.J. said.

5   Kellyann leaned towards me. "J.J.'s a jock. You know how they are," she said. She and Faith exchanged smiles. *No*, I thought, *I don't know how they are. Do guys who play sports eat a lot? Or a lot of pasta? Or red meat? What did she mean?* I didn't want to ask.

10   "I like your T-shirt," Faith said.

She was looking at my black 'Mt. Shasta' T-shirt with the rainbow-colored, snow-capped mountain.

"Thanks," I said, not really sure if she meant it.

"What's it mean?" Kellyann asked.

15   "It's a place. In California," I said.

"Um, okaaayyy," she said, like it was some mysterious abstract concept.

"I've heard of it. There's awesome snowboarding there. Right?" J.J. said, his mouth half full.

20   "Yeah!" I said, surprised.

People don't normally think of mountains when they think of California. Beaches, Hollywood, Silicon Valley – those are the usual clichés. They either forget or just don't know that the state has loads of mountains. Mt. Shasta is 25 as awesome as any mountain you'll see. It's also a sleeping volcano and a sacred place for Native Americans. That makes it extra awesome. Growing up in Weed, right next to Mt. Shasta, I felt that awesomeness every day. But nobody in Hartford had ever heard of Mt. Shasta – except J.J. That 30 earned him a few plus points in my book.

"I'd love to go to LA and Venice Beach," Kellyann sighed dreamily. "That would be sooo cool."

Like I said: clichés.

I still didn't understand why Kellyann and her friends were being so chatty with me. But did it matter why? For the first time at this school I felt included. Maybe I had judged these three too fast and too unfairly.

"Oh geez, look who just walked in," Kellyann groaned. I followed her eyes to the cafeteria entrance and saw Angel and her friend Latanya Freeman walking towards the lunch line. I knew Latanya from PE. Angel looked over at us, raising an eyebrow when she saw me.

"She's so cocky," Faith said.

"Yeah, like she owns the place," J.J. said.

A funny thing for you to say, I thought.

"That girl Latanya isn't much better. I mean, what kind of name is *La-tan-ya* anyway?" Kellyann said.

They all looked at each other and smiled. They looked at me, too, inviting me to share their joke. I didn't get it. I had my issues with Angel, but Latanya? We got along fine.

"You know," Kellyann said, putting a hand with polished fingernails on my arm, "the other day you did what you did for a reason, and I totally understand."

I wasn't sure what she was talking about. I noticed that she really did have the face of a model. Perfect proportions and carefully made-up. When had I ever used make-up like that? When had I ever used make-up at all? Her tidy blonde hair and her color-matched outfits made everything feel like it had an order and a purpose.

"Anyway, we've got your back," she said.

"Yeah, we support you," Faith said.

I still wasn't sure what this was about, but I didn't want them to think I was a total dummy.

"Aw, thanks, guys. That's so sweet," I said. Their faces softened. Kellyann looked at me like I was a puppy. Even J.J. gave
5 me a sweet smile.

"We have to stick together," Kellyann announced. "If we don't, they'll walk all over us." Faith and J.J. nodded.

Wait. We? They? I was completely confused. I tried to steer the conversation towards something I could understand.
10 "How's the bolognese?" I said to J.J.

"Awesome," he said, shoveling another oversized forkful into his mouth.

"Hey, next weekend we're going bowling," Kellyann said. "Why don't you come along?"

15 I was speechless. I still couldn't believe that we were having lunch together and now they were inviting me to hang out with them. On the weekend.

"Bowling? That sounds ... dope," I heard myself say. Full confession: In my view, bowling is definitely not dope. The
20 dumb shoes, the heavy bowling balls with the holes that never fit to your fingers, the artificial light, the noise, the stupid small talk. What's cool about it?

"Cool!" Kellyann said, smiling. "It'll be sooo much fun." She looked at the other two, who smiled and nodded.

25 I was in a daze as we carried our trays to the clean-up counter. *Did that just happen?* I thought. Kellyann said something about her locker and waved goodbye. The other two followed her. Leaving the cafeteria, I walked past the table where Angel and Latanya were having lunch. Tyrell Bailey, a
30 smooth-talking tenth-grader, was with them.

Latanya saw me and called out, "Hey, Iris." Angel looked around. I gave Latanya a wave and kept walking.

"Somebody's been making friends," Angel said loudly so that I'd hear it.

I didn't know where things were going with Kellyann, but ₅ did I care what Angel thought about it? I think you know the answer.

Chapter 7

It's funny how some things in your life don't seem like a big deal at first. Bryant Park was like that.

We were on the bus, coming home from school. Lalo was sitting in front of me, turned halfway around in his seat. Like most of the kids in the bus, he was in a Friday-afternoon mood – you know, relaxed and chatty. He was telling me about the *telenovelas* – the Spanish-language soap operas – that his mother watched passionately on cable TV. I could see that he loved them as much as his mom did. There was one called *Corazón Loco,* with lots of drama in it. A lot of the action in *Corazón Loco* took place in a city park that looks a lot like Bryant Park, he told me. The curious look on my face made him pause.

"Wait. You don't know about *Bryant Park*?" he asked. "Dios mío, chica, how long have you lived here?"

Lalo told me that Bryant Park was the only place in South End where kids our age could play and hang out without somebody calling the cops. He sounded like he spoke from experience.

I took his offer to be my tour guide, and the next day we walked the four blocks to the park. It was Saturday, late morning, and I had finally finished tidying my room, sweeping the front porch and taking out the trash.

Throwing on my jean jacket, I called to mom in the kitchen, "Enough of this. I'm running away from home and I'm never coming back!"

Mom knew me too well.

"Okay, have fun!" she said sweetly. "Don't forget the barbecue at three."

I didn't really want to think about the barbecue with Uncle Vinnie. Lalo was waiting at the corner of Bentley and Vine. We walked north along Bentley, then west along Sutter Avenue, past houses with big American flags, past a barking German Shepherd on a chain, past a pickup truck with a sticker on the back that said 'America – love it or leave it'. At the corner of Sutter and Franklin, the fruit stand in front of the Korean grocery store was busy with shoppers. Jason was wearing an apron and stacking melons. He saw us and smiled.

"Going to the park?"

"Yeah, Iris has never been there," Lalo said.

"You what?" Jason said, looking at me.

"Yeah, yeah, I'm the newbie. Get over it, guys," I said. They smiled at each other.

We crossed Franklin and continued along Sutter to the next block, where the sky suddenly opened up and there were trees and grassy areas and park benches. Bryant Park is one big city block. Part of it is green with a duck pond, a playground and picnic tables, another part is a concrete area for inline skaters and skateboarders, and beyond that are the basketball courts. That's where we went.

A group of girls were playing a full-court game on one court. On the other court we saw Tyrell. He was shooting baskets by himself. I only knew Tyrell because I'd seen him around school. He was tall like Lalo, but thinner and – okay, I'll say it – pretty good-looking. He wasn't the jock type, but he could play ball.

"Yo, what's up, Lalo?" Tyrell said, dribbling the ball between his legs.

"Hey Ty. Do you guys know each other?" Lalo said, sounding polite and grown-up.

5 "I've seen you around school. Iris, right?" Tyrell said to me. He took a jump shot and it swished through the net.

"Yep. I've seen you too," I said.

"Y'all want to play some?" he asked. Without waiting for an answer, he passed the ball to me. I caught it, stepped onto 10 the court and took a shot. It bounced off the backboard and went in.

"Ooh. This girl can play ball!" he said, smiling.

He passed the ball to Lalo. I knew Lalo wasn't a sporty guy. PE was his least favorite class. I was pretty sure he wouldn't 15 be interested. He looked awkward as he caught the ball and bounced it.

"Sure, let's play," Lalo said.

He had an eager smile I'd never seen on him. I wasn't used to playing with boys, especially two boys a lot bigger 20 than me, but I wasn't going to turn down a challenge. I threw my jean jacket on a courtside bench.

"What are we playing?" I said.

"How about two on two?" Tyrell said.

We were only three players. I looked at him.

25 "Yeah, yeah," he said. "We need one more."

On the other court, the girls were now standing around, talking and shooting.

"Yo, Latanya! We need you for two on two," he called.

I was surprised to see Latanya step out of the group.

She saw me and walked towards us. She was in short, cut-off jeans, a "Black Lives Matter" T-shirt and basketball shoes. Her hair was braided with colorful beads.

"Look who it is," she said smiling.

"I didn't recognize you with the braids," I said. 5

With another girl on the court, I felt better. We agreed on the teams – Tyrell and Latanya against Lalo and me. *This is going to be weird,* I thought.

A younger boy was standing next to the court, moving around restlessly, like he was waiting for something to hap- 10 pen. We started the game and he got excited, walking back and forth and clapping his hands. I recognized Matty in his behavior. He wasn't a Down kid, but he was special.

We played half-court. Tyrell and Latanya got the ball first. They passed it back and forth, looking for a shot. Lalo was 15 guarding Tyrell and I was on Latanya. From the start, Tyrell talked trash. A lot.

"Here it comes, Lalo," he said, dribbling the ball. "You can't stop it. Watch it now." He made a quick fake, slipped past Lalo and took the ball up for a smooth layup. Lalo looked 20 completely surprised.

"I told you. Didn't I tell you?" Tyrell teased.

Lalo smiled and shook his head. "Alright, I gave you that one," he joked.

I think I'm pretty good at reading people, but with Lalo 25 it wasn't easy. In my mind he wasn't someone who happily ran around a basketball court if he had the choice. Also, I expected the big guy to push back when someone tried to push him around. I was wrong on both counts.

"Come on, Lalo," I said. "Don't let him do that." I gave him 30 a high-five for support.

Tyrell passed the ball to Latanya. This time I got a hand on it and smacked it off the court and on to the grass. The boy cheered. He saw Latanya walk towards the ball and ran to get it first. He picked it up and ran away.

5 "Come on, Dion," she said. "Can I have it?"

"Give it up, Dion!" Tyrell yelled, slightly annoyed.

Each time Latanya got closer, he moved further away, smiling nervously. Finally he ran towards the court and launched the ball into the air from far away. It fell short of 10 the basket and Tyrell caught it on the bounce.

"Alright, you had your fun," Tyrell said to him.

The game went on and Lalo and I managed to get a basket each, but after about ten minutes we were losing 12–4 and I was getting tired of Tyrell's trash talk. He was having 15 too much fun teasing Lalo, who was no competition for him, and Lalo was taking it quietly. It was hard for me to watch. My ears started getting hot.

"Come and get the ball, big man," Tyrell said, dribbling the ball just out of Lalo's reach. "Come on! Here it is."

20 I moved towards Latanya near the top of the court, then went behind Tyrell, snatched the ball away and made a layup. Latanya laughed and Lalo watched, smiling.

"What was that, Tyrell?" Latanya teased.

Tyrell looked annoyed and embarrassed. "That wasn't 25 nothin'," he said.

"Maybe you shouldn't talk so much, *big man*," I said.

It was a dumb, hot-headed thing to do, I admit. He scored the next four baskets, and of course they won the game. But at least he didn't talk as much trash. Near the end, Lalo 30 missed one of my passes and the ball rolled onto the grass again. Dion ran and picked it up and started his routine. Latanya and Tyrell stood and watched this time.

I walked toward him, holding my hands out for the ball. He stepped further away and held the ball tightly in his arms with the same nervous smile. The situation felt oddly famil- 5 iar, so I did what I'd always done with Matty. I stood quietly, hands at my side, and looked at him. When he noticed I wasn't going to chase him, he slowly came closer, looking at the ground. I didn't move. Finally he tossed the ball to me and gave himself a hug. I felt like I knew him. 10

"You're Dion?" I asked. He nodded shyly.

"I'm Iris," I said.

"Iris," he said.

"Do you want to play? Take some shots?" I asked.

"Come on," Tyrell complained. "We ain't finished." 15

"Shut up, Tyrell," Latanya said.

Dion looked at me and shook his head.

"That's okay," I said, smiling. When I turned away, Dion ran up behind me, snatched the ball and did the same crazy long shot from the side of the court. This time it sailed 20 towards the hoop, hit the edge and bounced off. Lalo caught it and awkwardly layed it up into the basket.

"You did it, Dion!" he shouted.

"Oh my gosh, did you see that amazing shot?" I yelled, holding my head in my hands. 25

Dion laughed and ran around in circles, his arms stretched out like wings. Latanya chuckled.

"The winning basket!" Lalo said, arms in the air.

"Y'all didn't win nothin'," Tyrell said.

30

"Give me ten!" I said to Dion, holding my hands up. He lifted his hands and came closer, but pulled away at the last moment – just like Matty always did.

Lalo and I did a fist bump and laughed. There was more than one way to win a game.

Chapter 8

After the game, we exchanged fist bumps with Tyrell and
Latanya before they went on their way. Surprisingly, after all
the crap he got from Tyrell during the game, Lalo said goodbye to him like he was a dear friend. I didn't get it.

Lalo was still sweating and needed a rest, so we chilled ₅
on a park bench. I decided not to mention Tyrell just yet.
Instead I wondered about Dion, who had disappeared.

"Yeah, he's funny like that. One moment he's there, the
next he's gone," Lalo said.

Dion lived in the neighborhood and was known around ₁₀
the park, Lalo told me.

"Occasionally he has an episode. That's when you don't
want to be around him," Lalo said.

"Episode?" I said.

"Yeah. Something bothers him and he goes wild, scream- ₁₅
ing and thrashing around," he said. "Once he pushed and
kicked over a bunch of bikes and hurt himself. Another time
he tore through those flower beds over there." Lalo pointed
to a well-ordered bed of tulips. "He loses control and it takes
a while until he settles down. Then he's all smiles again. Like ₂₀
night and day."

It was like he was describing Matty, how he would sometimes be like a wild animal cut loose. I thought of the times
I'd had to somehow calm him down.

"You okay?" Lalo said. ₂₅

I looked at him. "Huh? Yeah. Just thinking about ... about Dion," I said.

We walked back along Sutter Avenue. After crossing Franklin at the busy traffic lights, we noticed Latanya and Tyrell
5 ahead of us, walking on the other side of the road.

"I don't know why you put up with Tyrell when he talks trash like that," I said.

"Aw, he doesn't mean it," Lalo said, looking in Tyrell's direction. "He likes me."

10 "He has a weird way of showing it," I said.

A police car rolled slowly past us. I could hear the crackle of the two-way radio inside the car. The car stopped slightly ahead of Tyrell and Latanya. Two police officers got out and stepped onto the sidewalk. They said something to Tyrell
15 and Latanya that we couldn't hear and the two stopped. Lalo stopped too.

"Oh, man. Here we go," he said.

"Huh?" I said.

Tyrell's and Latanya's serious faces told me the two police-
20 men weren't just saying hello. They seemed more interested in Tyrell. He shook his head and shrugged his shoulders. One policeman pointed at Tyrell's pockets.

"What are they doing?" I asked.

"It's called stop and search," Lalo said.

25 "Huh? Tyrell did something wrong?" I said.

"Nope. They don't need a reason," Lalo said. "They just look for any black or brown dude and stop him."

"What? That's crazy," I said. "Are you sure?"

"Just watch," Lalo said in a low voice.

The policeman who was talking to Tyrell was wearing mirrored sunglasses and had a tough-looking face. The other one stood beside Tyrell, like he wanted to make sure that Tyrell didn't run away. The one with the sunglasses pointed at the parked car next to them. Tyrell let the bas- 5 ketball fall to the ground. His shoulders slumped. He put his hands on the roof of the parked car and stood with his legs apart. The tough-looking cop began searching him, starting at his shoes and sliding his hands up each of his pant legs. He stopped at Tyrell's pockets and pulled out whatever 10 he could find, looking at it and laying it out on top of the car. The other officer started talking to Latanya. She looked upset. I could hear her saying "No!" and "Why? Why should I?" and "No, you ain't! Not with me!" The cop finally left her alone – maybe because she was a girl, and a pretty pissed- 15 off one too. The tough-looking cop finished his search and stepped back. Tyrell put his things back in his pockets. The cop stood watching him. I felt bad for Tyrell – it didn't matter how much trash he'd talked at the courts. He picked up his basketball. The tough cop said something to him. Then 20 Tyrell and Latanya quickly walked away.

"What did I tell you?" Lalo said, as we started walking.

The tough cop with sunglasses looked around. He saw us across the street and studied us for a moment. Then he and his partner got back in the patrol car. They continued down 25 the road and turned at the next corner.

"Whoa. What was that all about?" I said.

"You saw how he looked at us?" Lalo said. "He would have searched me, too, if you hadn't been here."

That sounded paranoid to me. "Come on. How do you 30 know that?" I said.

Lalo looked at me. "Are you serious? Because I'm not *white*, Iris," he said. His voice was hard.

We didn't talk for the rest of the way. I felt uncomfortable. Did he think I was just another white girl living in her
5 privileged white world? At the corner of Bentley and Vine, I wanted to say something.

"You're right. That sucked back there," I said weakly.

Lalo nodded. "Yup. Life in Hartford. See you in Social Studies, partner." He turned and walked away.

10 For once, Lalo had the last word.

"We're out here, Iris!" Mom called from the back yard. I was standing in the kitchen and could see them through the window – Mom and Dad and Uncle Vinnie and Aunt Gwen sitting around in lawn chairs with drinks in their hands.
15 "*There* she is!" Uncle Vinnie announced loudly as I stepped out the back door and sat down opposite them.

"There I am," I said, less enthusiastically.

"What have you been up to, Iris?" Dad asked.

"Basketball at Bryant Park," I said.

20 Uncle Vinnie nodded in approval. "Great park there. Nice place for you kids," he said.

"Bryant Park," Mom said. "Where is that? Did we go there as kids, Vinnie?"

"It didn't exist back then," he said. "It was a city project
25 about 15 years ago."

"Oh, right. Was it fun, Iris?" Mom asked.

I thought for a moment. "It was ... okay," I said.

"Just okay? What happened?" Aunt Gwen asked.

"The park was good," I said. "The walk home was a bit
30 weird." Uncle Vinnie the cop was sitting right in front of me,

but I couldn't stop myself. "Two kids from school got stopped
and searched." I felt Uncle Vinnie's eyes on me.

"What? By the police?" Dad said.

"Yeah. They were just walking home," I said.

Uncle Vinnie sat up in his chair. "I wouldn't worry about 5
that kind of thing, Iris. It was probably just a routine check,"
he said, sipping his beer.

"But they weren't doing anything wrong. Why did the
police stop them?" I asked him.

"Do you *know* they didn't do anything wrong?" he said. 10

"We played basketball together. Then they walked home.
That's all," I said.

"Like I said. Officers have to do routine checks sometimes. It keeps the streets safer," Uncle Vinnie said.

Mom looked uncomfortable. "Hey, how about we put that 15
meat on the grill?" she asked.

"Sure. Need some help?" Uncle Vinnie said, getting up.

Something still didn't feel right to me.

"Uncle Vinnie, how do you decide who to search and who
not to search?" I asked. 20

"Oh, you know, cops develop an eye for it," he said. "Let's
see if these coals are hot enough."

I couldn't let it go. "The two kids they stopped are black.
They could have stopped me, too, but they didn't," I said. "My
friend Lalo thinks it's because I'm white." 25

Uncle Vinnie turned to me. "Race has nothing to do with
it, Iris. Okay? Nothing."

Our eyes locked. The air suddenly got thick.

"I'm just trying to understand what happened," I said.

"Of course you are, sweetheart," Mom said. 30

They all began moving around, getting the barbecue and picnic table ready – anything to avoid a sensitive situation. Nobody noticed when I stood up and went back inside. From halfway up the stairs I could hear Mom.

5   "Iris, maybe you could help us with ... Iris? ... Where did she go?"

Chapter 9

In Mr. Wentworth's English class we're reading dystopian fiction. You know, stories about dark worlds where governments control people and life is totally screwed up. Monday morning felt dystopian to me. The memories of that cop searching Tyrell and the not-so-great conversation with Uncle Vinnie were still fresh in my mind.

When I walked into Social Studies, two police officers in full uniform were there, talking with Mrs. Jameson. The breakfast in my stomach suddenly felt like it wanted to go somewhere. One of them stood with his hands on his thick belt, the other one was sitting casually on the edge of the table. I don't know why their presence bothered me. My uncle is a cop, and what's wrong with cops anyway? But after Saturday I was beginning to think there were cops and then there were *cops*, if you know what I mean. I took a seat near the back and waited to find out which ones these two were. The last students drifted in and sat down.

"Let's get started," Mrs. Jameson said.

Lalo was three seats in front of me. The expression on his face told me he wasn't looking forward to this hour. He gave Jason in the next row a skeptical look. Angel, sitting three rows over and even further back, didn't look impressed either. Kellyann and J.J. sat up straight in their front-row seats looking eager and interested.

"Last Thursday we talked about anti-social behavior in its many forms," Mrs. Jameson said. "Today I'd like to introduce two guests – Officer Martinez and Officer Penrose from the Hartford Police Department. They've kindly taken time to come in this morning and talk to us about cyberbullying."

I'm sure there wasn't a single person in our class who didn't know about cyberbullying. Even if we hadn't all experienced it in texts or social media, we'd all heard and read enough about it. We knew it's not a good thing. We knew you shouldn't make it easy for other people to do it. So did we need some cops to talk to us about it? Officer Martinez stood up from the table.

"Hey guys, it's good to be here today," she started off. "Now, I know what you're thinking."

She was Latina and not very tall for a cop, but her confidence made up for it. She wore her hair tied neatly back and had amazingly white teeth and smooth brown skin. She looked relaxed and had a gentle smile. I could not picture her doing stop and search.

"You're thinking: what can a couple of cops tell you about cyberbullying that you don't already know, right?"

She got that right.

"You guys probably hear about it every day. Some of you experience it, I'm sure. Maybe some of you are cyberbullies yourselves," she said.

A few kids laughed nervously. Others looked around, smiling and shifting in their seats. Kellyann and J.J. exchanged whispers and giggles.

Officer Martinez smiled. "Don't worry, guys, we're not here to question anybody or make you feel uncomfortable."

I had to admit, she knew how to get the ball rolling. But what was the point of this?

"Officer Penrose and I are here to talk to you because cyberbullying is a lot more serious than most people think," she said.

Officer Penrose stood behind her, nodding his head. Then she surprised me.   5

"When I talk to *my* two kids about this, it worries me," she said. "They don't understand that cyberbullying can really hurt and even destroy people. I'm worried that it could happen to them. Or who knows? They could do it to someone else."   10

Wow, I thought. *She's not just a cop, she's a mom and she seems to really care about this stuff.*

When it was Officer Penrose's turn to talk, I expected a tougher message. It was hard not to look at the nightstick and the pistol in his heavy belt and to wonder how many   15
times he had used them. But when he spoke, he was more like a stand-up comedian than a hard-nosed street cop. His face and hands were expressive, like a stage actor. He did a cartoon-like imitation of a young bully texting mean thoughts. Even Mrs. Jameson smiled. Then he put us into groups. We   20
talked about the motivations behind bullying and presented and compared our ideas. This guy actually made a serious topic easier to discuss and even interesting. He was more like a teacher than a cop, to be honest.

The question-and-answer session afterwards was open   25
and lively. Even Lalo raised his hand a few times. When the bell rang, I was surprised how fast the time had gone by. Officer Martinez and Officer Penrose wished us well.

When we left the room, the skeptical look was gone from Lalo's face, and my day no longer felt so dystopian.   30

As you probably know, a school locker can be really useful, but only when it works. Mine didn't. I could open and close the door, but I couldn't lock the stupid thing. I had just gotten my books out for my next class and was trying to work the lock.

"Having trouble?"

I turned around and saw Jason. He looked relaxed with his rucksack slung over one shoulder.

"Maybe I'm just an idiot," I said. "I thought it's called a locker because you can lock it."

Jason laughed. "Yeah, makes sense, right? Can I try?"

I stepped aside. He put his rucksack down and started messing around with the lock and the door's moving parts. I felt like making conversation.

"You didn't make it to the park on Saturday," I said.

"Yeah, things got busy at the supermarket. It's often like that on Saturdays," he said.

"That kind of sucks, doesn't it?" I asked. "I mean Saturdays are for hanging out and doing fun stuff, right?"

I admit, I didn't know what I was trying to say. Jason looked at me and shrugged his shoulders.

"Not in my family," he said.

"Oh ... okay," I said.

Luckily, my dumb comment didn't seem to bother him.

"Lalo told me you guys were at the basketball courts. We should meet up and play some time," he said.

He seemed to really mean it. I smiled for the first time that day.

"That's a good –" I didn't finish my sentence.

"Hey, Lee, what's up, man?" J.J. said loudly.

He and Kellyann had appeared next to us.

Jason looked at him calmly. "Hey," he said.

From his cool reaction, I'd say Jason and J.J. weren't big buddies. Jason focused again on my locker.

"Hi Iris!" Kellyann said brightly. She looked at Jason. "What's he doing?" 5

"Trying to fix my locker. It won't lock," I said.

"Shhh," J.J. said, putting his finger to his lips and looking around. "Don't let anybody hear that."

I looked around. "I'm not too worried. It's not like I keep the family jewels in here or anything," I said. 10

J.J. and Kellyann laughed like I'd just told the funniest joke ever. Jason and I looked at each other.

"What did you guys think of Social Studies?" Kellyann asked. "Wasn't Officer Penrose awesome? She was kind of lame, though." J.J. nodded in agreement. 15

"Lame? Why?" I asked.

"Oh, you know, like the way she talked about her kids. Maybe it's a Mexican thing," she said. "I don't know why those people become cops."

I had no idea what she was trying to say. 20

"If you ask me, she looks like she ate too many tacos," J.J. said. "She probably couldn't catch a thief if she wanted to."

The two of them laughed quietly under their breath. They waited for us to laugh along with them, but I didn't see the humor. Jason clearly didn't want to be part of this conversa- 25 tion.

"I should get to class. Sorry about the locker," he said to me. "See you guys." He walked away.

Now it was the three of us and I missed Jason already.

"I thought they were okay," I heard myself say. "Not that I 30 think all cops are great."

The two of them looked puzzled.

"Hm. Anyway," Kellyann said. "I'm excited about Saturday. You too?"

My mind went blank. "Saturday?" I said.

5   "Bowling? Hello? Have you forgotten?" she said.

I quickly remembered. "Oh! Right. I wasn't thinking."

Mr. Barnes's booming voice suddenly cut through the hallway noise. "Let's move it along, people!"

Kellyann and J.J. disappeared as quickly as they'd come.
10 I gathered my books, shut my locker door and turned to go. My eyes immediately met Angel's. She was standing across the hallway with another girl. It looked like she'd been watching us.

"Hm," she said disapprovingly. "Some people don't seem
15 to care who they hang out with."

My ears went hot. "Some people should mind their own business," I shot back and walked away.

"I *know* what *my* business is," I heard her say.

Yeah, sure you do, I thought.

Chapter 10

Let's be clear about something: I hate work. School work, homework, house chores, garden work – it all sucks. But I'll be honest: sometimes it's useful.

Mae couldn't believe what she'd just heard.

"Are you sure? I don't want you to get any dirt under those clean fingernails of yours," she said, chuckling. 5

If I hadn't been in such a terrible mood, maybe I would have laughed too.

"Hey, I'm offering my help," I said. "You should take it while you can get it." 10

It wasn't really work that I was looking for. I knew I could share my thoughts with Mae and she'd listen and comment in that old-lady kind of way. Sometimes that was all I needed. But I knew that Mae doesn't like to sit around. Visiting her always had a price. 15

"Ain't no shortage of things to do here," she said. "You can start by helping me get the apples off this tree."

I hadn't noticed the old tree next to her house. It was full of apples in different shades of green, yellow and red. Mae had already started filling an old plastic bucket. 20

"Let's do it," I said.

We started picking the apples and the bucket filled up fast. Then Mae put a ladder up next to the tree.

"You can get up there better than I can," she said, looking up at the higher branches. 25

I shrugged and climbed up the ladder. There were apples everywhere. I picked and handed them down.

"I know you didn't just come here to work, Iris Quinn," Mae said. "What's on your mind?"

⁵ She knew how to read me. I thought for a moment.

"Do you care what people think of you?" I asked.

"Now that's an interesting question," she said. "I guess it depends on who the people are."

"Should it bother me if people who I don't really know or ¹⁰ care about have a wrong impression of me?" I asked.

"Listen, child," she said. "When most people on this street look at me, they see a crazy old black lady who talks to herself in her overgrown garden. They don't want nothin' to do with me. But do I look like I care?"

¹⁵ "You mean ... you're not crazy?" I asked.

Mae laughed loudly. Soon we were both laughing.

"Be careful up there," she said, holding the ladder with both hands. She caught her breath. "Oh, Lord. Sometimes I wish I was. Crazy, I mean."

²⁰ I passed some more apples to her.

"The thing is, I don't know a lot of people here," I explained. "And the one girl who wants me to be her friend is ... different."

"Different ain't always a bad thing," Mae said.

²⁵ "What I mean is that she's not always very nice," I said. I thought for a moment. "Actually, I'm not either."

"Maybe you're more like her than you think," she said.

"No," I said. "I'm not like her."

"You're not making sense, Iris Quinn," she said.

³⁰ I kept picking. Another thought came.

"The other day I saw two white policemen stop and search two black kids from school. They hadn't done anything wrong. I can't stop thinking about that," I said.

Mae rubbed an apple on her tattered old sweater.

"Yeah, that happens," she said. "Are you changing the subject now?" 5

"I wonder if people at school think I'm racist," I said.

"Why? Are you racist?" Mae asked with a chuckle.

"I don't know. I hope not," I said.

Mae looked up at me. "That's as honest an answer as I've ever heard." 10

I passed two more apples to her.

"We need another bucket. This one's full," she said.

I climbed down the ladder and helped her carry the full bucket of apples to the kitchen door. 15

"Not all police are good. There are definitely some bad apples out there," she said, chuckling at her own joke. She stared at the tree, shaking her head.

"I tell you, when people don't respect others it hurts everybody, one way or another. That's God's truth." 20

"Maybe they should all come to Mae's garden," I said.

Mae smiled. "I'd put them all to work, you can be sure of that!"

The garage door was open when I got home and Dad was in the garage. I went to see what he was doing. 25

"There's too much stuff in here. I think we can organize it better," he told me.

He was pulling out car tires, chairs, suitcases and other stuff and sorting it on the grass in the backyard. The barbecue stood nearby, cold and empty. I stared at it. 30

"What did you think about what Uncle Vinnie was saying the other day?" I asked.

"About what?" Dad asked.

"About how the police stop and search people," I said.

5 "I think he thought you were suggesting that the police only stop black and Latino kids," he said. "That's a touchy subject, Iris. After all, Uncle Vinnie is a cop."

"Are you saying you agree with him?" I asked.

"No. I'm saying that you can't–"

10 "So you don't agree with him," I said.

Dad sighed. "'Stop and frisk' is what they call it, and yes, it's controversial in some cities. No question. I've read statistics from New York City. Ninety percent of the kids they stopped there were ... not white. And 70 percent of them
15 hadn't done anything wrong," he said.

"Wow," I said. "So it's true."

"I said *in some cities*, Iris. We don't know what it's like here in Hartford," he said. "And I don't think you should push this too much with your Uncle Vinnie."

20 "But you two don't agree on everything either," I said.

"That's okay, Iris. He's my brother-in-law. He's ... family," he said. It sounded like the word didn't sit comfortably in his mouth.

"So it's okay that he thinks that way because he's family?"
25 I asked.

Dad scratched his beard.

"And you can disagree with him but I shouldn't?"

"That's not what I'm saying, Iris."

"Maybe Mom takes his point of view only because he's
30 her brother."

He was silent. I had thrown too much at him.

"You know what?" he said, "I think you and Uncle Vinnie can sort this out just fine without me." He went back into the garage. I watched him go.

When I was a little kid, Dad liked to call me "Miss Mouth" because I always argued and couldn't shut up. He doesn't call ₅ me that anymore, but sometimes, like now, I think it's clear to us both that the nickname still fits.

Chapter 11

There are situations when Matty is my best teacher. That probably sounds weird. What can you learn from an eight-year-old kid with Down Syndrome, right? But you didn't know my little brother. Matty saw things that other people
5 didn't see. Everything was interesting to him. Everything had some kind of meaning.

Like he could laugh his head off at a flock of starlings racing around the sky. He liked taking photos of snails, shadows, dirty windows and old shoes. In foot races with other kids,
10 he usually came in last place, but it didn't matter to him. He was all smiles. It was one big thrill to him. That's how he was with everything – he was all in, all the time. It was hard work for Mom and Dad. It's what made him hop on his bike and race down the street that day. It's what cost him his life. And
15 it's what I'm still trying to learn from him.

Sitting in Social Studies, I felt like I needed some of that wide-eyed enthusiasm of Matty's. The topic was still the civil rights movement and the day had come when Lalo and I had to present our report on the Freedom Rides. Maybe I would
20 have felt more motivated if things had been better between Lalo and me. But since that day when the cops searched Tyrell, Lalo had been less interested in me. It seemed like I was now the typical white girl who didn't understand the problems of disadvantaged people of color.

We had talked about our report and who would present what. But we hadn't practiced anything, and neither of us had any idea what the other one was going to say.

Fantastic, I thought to myself. *We are going to crash and burn in front of the whole class.*   5

It didn't help that Kellyann and Faith had just delivered a perfect report. They were so organized it was ridiculous. Their topic was the Greensboro Sit-in of 1960, a non-violent protest against racial segregation. A group of black students had sat down at a whites-only lunch cafe and refused to   10
leave. Kellyann and Faith had an impressive slideshow with photos, maps, front pages of newspapers and even background music. Everything was amazingly timed and choreographed. With extra make-up and her hair neatly tied back, Kellyann looked like one of those picture-perfect TV news   15
presenters. Faith had memorized her notes and was using her hands to gesture and point to the slides. There was no way we could beat that.

When Faith asked the class at the end if there were any questions, J.J. raised his hand.   20

"Was the sit-in really totally non-violent? I've read that some of the students were arrested by the police," he said.

Kellyann nodded. "That's true. Sadly, a lot of them didn't behave well. So it's not surprising that they were arrested," she said.   25

A few people shifted in their seats, including Lalo. "Maybe the police were looking for reasons to arrest them," he said without raising his hand.

"Yeah. What would you have done in their situation?" someone else shouted.   30

I thought Angel would say something, but when I looked around, she wasn't there.

Mrs. Jameson stood up quickly. "Thank you, Kellyann and Faith. We'll have to end it there."

5 Kellyann looked surprised, like she wasn't ready to give up her moment in the spotlight. She shuffled back to her seat.

"Iris and Lalo, are you ready?" Mrs. Jameson asked.

Definitely not, I thought. I sighed, stood up and walked to the front of the room. I'd decided I was going to jump right in

10 and hope for the best. Lalo went straight to the smartboard and started setting up the slideshow he had organized. He looked more confident than I felt. I decided not to wait for him. I cleared my throat.

"Our report today is about the Freedom Rides."

15 I had on my signature black T-shirt and faded jeans. Lalo was in a blue, long-sleeved shirt, buttoned all the way up and hanging big and loose over his black sweatpants. We were a stark contrast to Kellyann and Faith.

"The Freedom Rides were a series of non-violent protests

20 in the South in 1961," I continued, trying not to read from my notes. "African-American and white activists wanted to challenge state laws in the South that said whites and blacks couldn't use the same facilities in interstate bus stations. So they rode buses together in groups from state to state. When

25 they stopped at a bus station, the white Freedom Riders used the blacks-only toilets, waiting rooms and cafes, and the black Freedom Riders used the whites-only ones."

I paused and looked at Lalo, not sure if I should continue. He must have thought it was a signal because he tapped

30 the smartboard with his fingers. A color map of the South

appeared. I had no idea where he got it, but it looked good to me.

Lalo suddenly came to life. "This map shows the first four Freedom Rides, the cities where they started and finished, and the stops along the way," he said, pointing at different colored lines on the map.

He tapped the board again and the next slide showed a photo from that time. Two men, one of them black, the other white, with blood on their clothes and faces.

"The Freedom Riders were attacked by white racists at stops along the way. The local police didn't do much to stop the attacks. A lot of the Riders were arrested and jailed," Lalo said. "In Alabama, one of the first buses was stopped by a mob of angry white men and set on fire. When the Riders managed to escape the bus, the mob outside beat them with sticks and pipes and chains."

Lalo tapped the board and a black-and-white photo of a burning bus appeared. You could see people standing and lying near the bus. They looked confused. Some of them looked injured. The whole class was still.

Lalo showed more photos. He waited for the dramatic images to have their effect. He looked at me and nodded, like he was saying, "I've got this." We had two more minutes to finish. I had no idea what to do next, but Lalo seemed to have a plan, so I kept my mouth shut.

"These activists knew they'd face strong resistance and sometimes horrible violence, but it didn't stop them," he said. "They knew that if they stopped, if they let the white racists think they were afraid, then the racist laws would continue. So they organized even more Freedom Rides."

Then he read from his notes. "May 17th to May 21st –
Washington, D.C. to New Orleans, Louisiana. May 24th to
May 25th ..." He named every Freedom Ride that followed.

Lalo tapped the board again and again. Police mugshots
of the arrested students appeared, one after another. Female
and male, black and white, looking straight into the cam-
era. The activists had been normal people, but the police had
treated them like criminals. Their different faces told different stories. One black girl's face caught my attention. Her
eyes seemed to reach out and touch me.

They all looked like they knew what they were doing and
why. Something clicked in my head. Suddenly I knew why we
were doing this. I looked around. Lalo had everyone's attention. He had brought the story to life. He understood the
events in a way that I hadn't before, but now it made sense. I
looked at my notes and stepped forward.

"The Rides continued for six months. Over 60 Freedom
Rides took place all over the Southern states and hundreds
of student activists took part," I said. I didn't need my notes
anymore. I described how the violence and the arrests
shocked the nation, how the world followed what was going
on, how Kennedy and his government had to do something,
how they pressured the Southern states, and how new laws
in September 1961 finally ended the segregation of interstate
buses and bus stations. I could have ended our presentation
there, but I knew Lalo should do it. I looked over at him and
his eyes lit up.

"After that, anybody could travel freely on interstate
buses and trains, and the 'white' and 'colored' signs disappeared from bus and train stations across the South," he
said, his voice getting stronger. "The Freedom Rides inspired

people all over the country to take part in other kinds of direct action. It was an important victory for civil rights and against racism," he concluded. "Thank you."

We answered a few questions and I saw Kellyann's eyes looking around like she was getting ready to ask something, but she stayed quiet. Mrs. Jameson was smiling. Returning to our seats, Lalo passed my desk. He gave me a fist bump. We had given an awesome presentation and that felt good, but the fist bump felt even better. I don't know why, but I thought of Angel and wished she had been there.

Maneuvering through the crowded hallway on my way to Woodworking class, I saw Lalo's big figure ahead of me. He was standing with his locker door open. It was a good chance to talk to him, but his attention was across the hallway, where a boy was reaching down into a locker. When the boy straightened up, I saw it was Tyrell. He didn't see that Lalo was watching him. At first I didn't understand. Then it hit me.

I can be naive about some things, I admit. But I know when someone is checking someone out, and I don't mean just being curious. I stopped in the middle of the hallway. Kids were bumping into me and trying to go around me.

Why hadn't I noticed it before? The way Lalo was looking at Tyrell explained so much – especially his behavior at Bryant Park. I thought of my friend Dane Riley back in Weed. In eighth grade, Dane wasn't ready to come out, but he had eyes for a guy in our homeroom and he wasn't good at hiding it. Maybe it was similar with Lalo. I wanted to talk to him about it but knew I couldn't.

"I get it now," I said, walking up to him.

Lalo looked at me like a kid who'd just been caught with his hand in the cookie jar.

"Wh–What do you mean?" he said.

"I understand what you were talking about that day – you
5 know, about the cops," I said.

I could see that his thoughts were moving slowly.

"Anyway, I'm glad we did that presentation together. You were amazing," I said. I think he saw that I meant it. His big face softened and a gentle smile began to spread.

10 "We were pretty awesome, weren't we?" he said.

Behind Lalo I could see Kellyann making her way down the busy hallway, looking neat and perfect in every way. You didn't have to like her to be impressed. She pretended not to see me. I think that's so weird when kids do that.

15 "Hey, Kellyann," I said as she passed us. She acted surprised.

"Oh, hi!" she said.

"You guys were good," I said.

"Huh? Oh, that," she said. "Yeah, it wasn't that hard," she
20 said. "It's a shame we didn't have a more interesting subject."

She looked Lalo up and down but avoided eye contact.

"Anyway, I don't know why they make such a big deal about that stuff," she said.

"What stuff?" I asked.

25 She turned her back to Lalo and leaned in close to me, like we were sharing a secret.

"Those 'sit-ins' and 'Freedom Rides' and stuff," she said. "You know what I mean, right?" She rolled her eyes.

Lalo had finished getting his books out of his locker. He
30 stood quietly, looking like he wanted to leave.

"It's like all this Black Lives Matter stuff," she said, low-ering her voice. "Why are they so special? I mean, don't *all* lives matter?"

Wow, I thought. *Hopefully Lalo didn't hear that.* I remem-bered Dad's words to Mom. Kellyann was finally showing her true colors and they weren't pretty. She waited for my reaction, her eyes fixed on me.

"I don't know what you're talking about," I said.

I could see she hadn't expected that. Her eyes got big.

"Well, think what you like," she said finally.

I wasn't sure what else to say.

"Anyway, we're meeting at the bowling alley tomorrow at seven-thirty," she said. "You're coming, right?"

It sounded more like a command than a question. She fixed her eyes on me again. I looked at Lalo, who was getting ready to leave.

"Actually, I have other plans," I said. The answer came easi-ly and it felt right. She looked uncomfortable.

"Fine. Do what you like," she said, giving me a cold look before turning away. She waved her manicured fingers in the air without looking back.

"See ya," I said.

After she'd gone, Lalo found his voice again. "Man, what an ice queen. What did I ever do to her?"

"Probably nothing," I said. "I really wouldn't worry about it."

Chapter 12

The next day started like most Saturdays. When the chores were done and the day was mine, it didn't take long before I was bored. This time I decided to see what was up at Bryant Park.

5   When I arrived at the courts, a mixed bunch of kids were shooting baskets – different ages and social groups, guys and girls, mostly African-American, some Latino, a few Asian and, counting me, only two white kids. Basketball – the great uniter. I knew some of the kids from school. Jason was there,

10 happy to be done with work, making long jump shots and quick, smooth layups. I had wondered if he was good. Now I could see it. Tyrell was there too, talking and joking between dribbles and shots. I didn't see Latanya. But someone else was at the other end of the court: Angel. Part of me wanted

15 to turn around and go home. But the other part gave me a kick in the butt.

Don't let her stop you from being here, I thought.

Then someone called my name. "Hey, Iris!"

I turned and saw Dion smiling from the other side of the

20 court. His oversized, white T-shirt and baggy shorts contrasted with his thin, dark arms and legs. He had on huge basketball shoes. He looked sweet and cartoon-like with his wide, toothy smile that made his ears stick out.

"Hey there, Dion," I said.

25 Angel turned around and looked at Dion and then at me. She seemed puzzled. *It's none of your business,* I thought. She

must have read my face, because she went back to shooting baskets.

It didn't take long before two teams of five players had formed and we had a full-court game going. Most of the girls didn't want to play with so many boys and moved to the other court. I didn't mind. It looked like Angel didn't either. We both made sure we weren't on the same team.

The game started fast with a lot of running and shooting. Most of the boys weren't used to playing with girls. I had to yell at them to pass me the ball. Luckily, Jason was on my team. After Tyrell scored a long jumper, I brought the ball in.

"Iris!" Jason called.

He was at half-court and running two steps ahead of the kid who was guarding him. I threw the ball down the court. He caught it on the bounce and made a beautiful layup before the other kid could get close.

"Nice one," he said as he ran back up the court.

Angel showed a few moves of her own, blocking one of Jason's layups and making a turn-around jump shot. I already knew she was dangerous; the guys were just finding out.

The game turned into a duel between Tyrell and Angel on one team and Jason and me on the other. The other kids weren't doing much. Dion was in his cheerleader role, running up and down the sideline.

I didn't want to get into it with Angel, but it bothered me that the guys on our team didn't know how to stop her. After she grabbed an easy rebound, she relaxed with the ball for a moment. I slapped it out of her hand, grabbed it on the bounce and passed it inside to Jason, who laid the ball up for another two points. Dion went wild.

"Yeah, Iris!" he cheered, jumping and spinning around. Angel looked at him, annoyed.

"Be quiet, Dion," she said.

His smile disappeared. Then he covered his mouth with his hand and giggled. Angel shook her head.

It was a close game. Tyrell talked trash as usual, but when Jason scored against him, he showed respect. Watching Tyrell, I wondered what he would think if he knew how Lalo felt about him.

Jason passed the ball to me and I dribbled around one of the guys. Angel was there waiting for me and snatched the ball away.

"Yeah!" Tyrell yelled. Dion clapped his hands.

She dribbled away from me, looking satisfied with herself. My ears were like two hot potatoes. I chased after the ball, but with her long arms she had no problem keeping it away from me. I fouled her at least twice while trying to get the ball back.

"Don't start that now," she said to me, annoyed.

"Start what?" I said.

"You *know* what," she said.

Suddenly a loud siren cut through the cool autumn air. WhhoooooooOOOOoooooo...

Everyone stopped and turned. A police car with flashing blue lights was speeding in our direction along the street next to the park. A distant memory of sirens and flashing lights gave me a heavy feeling. I looked over at Tyrell across the court. He stood still, his face tense and serious. The police car got closer and louder. Then, almost without slowing down, it turned onto a side street and was gone, its siren getting more and more distant.

"Man, that was loud," someone said.

Tyrell tried to act like nothing had happened, but I could see that he was shaken.

I heard Angel. "Where's Dion?"

We all looked around.   5

"He was just here," Jason said.

Something made my heart beat faster and I quickly scanned the park. I spotted him under a picnic table with his legs pulled to his chest and his arms wrapped around tightly. His face was buried between his knees.   10

"There," I said. I ran to him and some of the others followed. He was shaking. The siren had freaked him out.

"Dion, it's okay," I said to him, moving closer. Then Angel stepped in front of me and bent down next to him.

"Dion, come on, it's over. It's nothing," she said, like she   15
knew what was going on. She reached under the table and put her hand on his head. Dion looked up and there was real fear in his face. He seemed relieved to see Angel.

"Come on out," she said gently.

Dion took Angel's hand and slowly climbed out from   20
under the table. He wrapped his thin arms tightly around her waist and she put her arm around his shoulders. Now I understood why Angel had been acting the way she had. Nobody had told me that she and Dion were sister and brother.   25

"Let's go home," she said to him. "See y'all," she said, looking over her shoulder.

I watched them walk slowly across the park. Just a minute before, I had felt as far apart from Angel as I ever had. Now it felt like something connected us.   30

Chapter 13

I think we can agree on one thing: Monday mornings suck. This Monday morning, though, was suckier than most. It was my first class. Woodworking with Mr. Rashad. On Mondays it's also homeroom, so Mr. Rashad was handing out informa-
5 tion about important school dates. He had just put a photocopy on my desk when a voice came over the loudspeaker. It was Mrs. Gupta, the school secretary.

"Good morning. Would Iris Quinn, grade nine, please report to the main office? Iris Quinn, please report to the
10 main office. Thank you."

The whole class turned and looked at me. "Ooh, that's you, Iris," someone said. Some students whispered and mumbled to each other.

Mr. Rashad looked over. "You'd better find out what that's
15 all about, Iris," he said. "And the rest of you can be quiet while I finish handing these out."

I had no idea what Mrs. Gupta wanted from me, but I had the feeling it wasn't good. Walking down the quiet, empty hallway, some possible scenarios went through my
20 head. Maybe it was a call from home. Maybe something terrible had happened, like Mom or Dad had had an accident. I couldn't imagine that it had anything to do with school, since nothing bad had happened since the cafeteria incident.

The door to the main office was open and I walked in.
25 Mrs. Gupta was busy at her computer. She looked up.

"Oh, Iris, there you are. You can go straight in," she said, gesturing towards Mr. Barnes's office.

I turned and saw Dad through the open door, sitting on the chair I had sat on the week before. He was talking and his face looked serious. *Geez,* I thought, *maybe something really has happened to Mom.* I walked into the principal's office. Mr. Barnes looked up.

"Miss Quinn, sit down, please," he said.

He got up from his squeaky office chair, slid another chair over near Dad's and closed the door.

"Is everything okay?" I asked Dad. "What's going on?"

Dad looked like he wanted to ask me the same. I was confused. I looked at Mr. Barnes. His face was as serious as ever.

"Miss Quinn, last week I explained to you our three-strikes-and-you're-out rule. Do you remember?" he said.

"How could I forget?" I said.

He stared at his desk, like he was waiting for something.

"I don't understand," I said. "What's up?"

Mr. Barnes stood up and turned to the window. "I asked you here because of what happened out there," he said.

He pointed. I looked out and saw the empty school court-yard and, on the far end, the colorful side wall of Building B. Some art students years ago had painted a huge, beautiful wall mural to celebrate the school's multiculturalism. I was still confused.

"Sorry, what are you–?" Before I got to the end of my sentence, I saw it. I stood up to get a better view. The wall mural had been spray-painted over with big messy white letters that said, "ALL LIVES MATTER." My mouth dropped open. Mr. Barnes looked at me.

"You look surprised, Miss Quinn," he said.

He was looking straight at me with that raised eyebrow of his that said, "Don't try to fool me."

"You think that I did that?" I said.

Dad seemed like he wasn't sure what to do or say or think.
5 Neither of them spoke.

"No way," I said. "Not me. Why would I do that?"

Mr. Barnes stood with his hands on his hips. He reached for something on the floor and lifted it onto his desk. It was a gym bag. I looked at it twice.

10 "That's mine," I said.

"I know. Your name is written on the inside," he said.

"Where'd you get it?" I asked. "And why are you showing that to me?"

Mr. Barnes looked at Dad, who seemed to already know
15 the answer. Dad looked down at his hands, then up at me.

"One of our administrators found it outside near Building B," Mr. Barnes said. "The things in there seem to tell a different story."

He held the bag open. There were several used cans of
20 white spray paint and some gloves. I stared at the stuff, trying to understand. It was too crazy to believe, but there it was. And Mr. Barnes and Dad seemed to believe it.

No matter how many ways I tried to tell them I had nothing to do with the graffiti, Mr. Barnes wasn't buying it. Dad
25 seemed sympathetic. He really wanted to believe that my gym bag full of white spray paint had found its way out there without my help, but I could see it was hard for him. My ears were steaming. Finally I exploded.

"What do you even know about me?" I shouted at Mr.
30 Barnes. "Do you even care? All you care about is this stupid school!"

"It is my job to care about this school," he said quietly, as he wrote some notes down on a notepad.

Then the tears came. I didn't want to cry in front of them, especially not in front of Mr. Barnes, but maybe you know how it is: once it starts, it's hard to stop it. First the tears, 5 then the snot running out of your nose. It probably looked pretty gross. Dad handed me a tissue and I blew my nose loudly. Then I decided I'd had enough.

"I'm done with this," I said, wiping the tears away. "You can think what you want. I'm going back to class." 10

I stood up. I had no idea what I was doing. How could I go back to class looking the way I did?

"We're not done, Miss Quinn," Mr. Barnes said calmly.

Don't you hate it when grown-ups stay calm while you're flipping out about something? 15

"Please sit down, Iris," Dad said.

"Why?! This is a joke!!!" I screamed. A river of tears and snot flowed freely again.

"Please keep your voice down," Mr. Barnes said firmly. His eyes got big. "And *sit down*," he said. 20

I should note here that Mr. Barnes is a big guy with a serious face and a deep voice like Barack Obama's. He knows how to get respect. I sat back down.

"Now. Until I find out what's going on, this is Strike Two against you," he said. 25

Wow, I thought. I knew the "Strike Two" part was coming, but I didn't expect the part before that. It sounded like he was keeping an open mind. Maybe I could still convince him.

"But let me make this clear," he continued, "you are Suspect Number One, Miss Quinn, and right now I don't see any other suspects," he said.

Forget about the open mind, I thought.

5 As we left Mr. Barnes's office, Dad rested his hand on my shoulder, "We'll talk about this when you get home."

I didn't say anything. *Yeah, I'm sure we will,* I thought.

The rest of the school day was a blur. People talked the whole day about the graffiti. Understandably, the Afri-
10 can-American students were especially pissed off. I didn't talk to anybody except Lalo, and that was in the school bus coming home. I told him about my meeting with Mr. Barnes and about the gym bag.

"What? I can't believe it! Who would do that?" he said.

15 At least I had one person on my side.

At dinner that evening, Dad seemed to soften a bit. He probably realized his job was to believe and support his daughter. At least, that's what I'd like to think. Mom was having trouble understanding the situation.

20 "What are all these people upset about? Is it the mural? *That* I can understand," she said.

Dad looked at her. "It's more than that, Bianca."

"I still don't get how your gym bag got mixed up in all this," Dad said to me.

25 "I don't either!" I said. Then, like a lightning flash, it hit me. "Wait! My locker. It doesn't work. I can't lock it."

Dad and I looked at each other. Mom looked confused.

"Will you *please* tell me what's going on?" she said.

They say lightning never strikes twice in the same place, but it did this time. I stood up suddenly.

"I gotta make a phone call," I said. Mom and Dad looked puzzled. I went out to the back yard with my phone. Lalo answered after one ring. 5

"Hola," he said.

"Lalo. Last week I couldn't lock my locker because the freaking lock wasn't working. Jason was there. Then Kellyann and J.J. showed up and saw what was going on. Dude, my gym bag was *in my locker*," I said. 10

"Whoa, hold on," he said. "Are you saying Jason–?"

"No! Not Jason. Kellyann and J.J.! J.J. even made a dumb joke about it." I didn't hear anything. "Lalo? Are you still there?"

"Yeah," he said finally. "I'm thinking about what Kellyann 15 said in the hallway. Remember? She didn't want me to hear it, but of course I heard it."

I didn't have to think hard. "You mean, 'Don't all lives matter?'"

"That's it." 20

It all made sense. That was on Friday. Kellyann and I had disagreed.

"Do you think they really–?"

"Oh yeah. Listen, Iris, you need to move fast on this."

"But how can I prove it?" 25

"Let me think about that. I gotta go now. *Corazón Loco* starts in two minutes."

Chapter 14

We met in the hallway outside the cafeteria. It was the first time I had seen Lalo that day and he looked different. He was wearing black jeans instead of his usual baggy sweatpants. The jeans had a better cut and made him look sportier. He had on a plain white T-shirt and a green bomber jacket. It looked good.

"Hey, look at you!" I said. "I like it."

"I felt like I needed a change," he said.

There was something else about him. His hair was freshly cut and neatly combed and the tiny stud that you could hardly see in his right ear was now a silver ring that seemed to say "look at me". It was all part of a process I had noticed. Lalo was showing himself. It was nice to see.

"Are you sure you want to do this?" I asked.

"There's nothing else I'd rather do," he said.

I was nervous, but I badly wanted to sort this out. Maybe Lalo's idea wasn't the best, but it was the only one we had. We walked in and scanned the cafeteria.

"There," Lalo said, looking at a table on the left side.

As soon as I saw them, my ears began doing their thing. I took a deep breath. *Let's play this cool,* I thought. Kellyann and J.J. were sitting next to each other and didn't notice when we walked up to the table.

"Hey, is that vegetarian lasagna?" I said to Kellyann. "That's my favorite too. Isn't that funny?"

They both looked up, surprised. We sat down opposite them. J.J. had his mouth full of food. He looked at Lalo like he was from another planet. Lalo looked back at him.

"Hola," he said. Neither of them reacted.

"How was the bowling on Saturday?" I asked, not really interested in their answer. 5

"You missed it. It was awesome," J.J. said.

Kellyann gave me a cold stare. "I heard you got into trouble," she said. "Something about some graffiti?"

I let her enjoy the moment. "Yeah," I said. "The principal thinks I painted over the wall mural. They found a bag of mine with spray paint in it. I can't explain it." 10

I paused for a bit of dramatic effect, then looked straight at both of them.

"You don't know anything about that, do you?" I asked. 15

J.J. looked wide-eyed and shrugged his shoulders. Kellyann put on her best innocent face.

"Me? I don't know anything about any graffiti. Or your gym bag," Kellyann said.

Lalo and I looked at each other. 20

"Sorry, did you just say 'gym bag'?" I said. "What makes you think I'm talking about my gym bag?"

Kellyann's eyes searched around. "Did I say gym bag?"

I turned to J.J. "She did say gym bag, didn't she?" He looked at me with a stone face. 25

"I definitely heard gym bag," Lalo said.

"Who asked you, gay-boy?" J.J. said, his voice hard.

His words surprised me. I wondered how Lalo felt. Was it the first time someone had said that to him? Lalo's reaction was beautiful. He smiled. 30

"I don't need your permission to talk, white-boy."

I looked at Kellyann. "I think you know more about that graffiti than you say you do," I said calmly.

Kellyann looked surprised. She knew the game was over. Her glossy lips tightened. Her face got red with anger that no ⁵ amount of make-up could hide.

"Maybe," she said. "Maybe you deserved it. Anyway, it's true what it says on the wall, so what's the problem?"

J.J. smiled. "Don't you like my handwriting?" he said.

I sat back. "Wow. So you're both admitting it."

¹⁰ "We're not admitting anything," Kellyann said.

"Nope," J.J. said.

"I just heard you," I said. "And Lalo is my witness."

"Yup," Lalo said.

Her cold, blue eyes drilled into me. "Well, J.J. is my witness ¹⁵ and I'm his. You can't prove it," she said. "So get your thin ugly butt out of here and take fat-boy with you."

Why had I ever thought she was pretty? "At least I don't try to cover mine up with cheap make-up," I said.

Her face went tomato red. Her eyes nearly popped out of ²⁰ her head. I could feel what was coming next.

"You little shit," she said. "Here's your freaking vegetarian lasagna."

Her fingers curled around the sides of her lunch tray and with one quick movement she tried to dump her lunch on ²⁵ me. Luckily, I knew more about tray aerodynamics than she did. I blocked the tray with both hands and everything on it flew back at her. The plate, cutlery, dessert dish and the tray itself crashed loudly onto the table and floor. The cafeteria went silent. All eyes were on Kellyann. She's normally some-³⁰ one who likes attention, but I think this time was different. Tomato sauce and mozzarella cheese were on her face and all down her neat, expensive blouse. The rest of her lasagna was sitting warmly in her lap. She looked shocked, her mouth hanging open.

"My blouse!!!" she squealed. "What the hell?!!!"

J.J. stood up and tried to pour his chocolate milk on me. Lalo reached out and grabbed his arm. J.J. couldn't move. Lalo was not only bigger than him, he was stronger. I could see the pain in J.J.'s face. With his other hand, Lalo took the milk carton out of J.J.'s hand.

"Now *sit your butt down*," he said firmly.

The pain was too much for J.J. and he sat down slowly. Lalo finally let go of his arm.

The next voice I heard was Mrs. Gonzalez's.

Mr. Barnes's office had begun to feel familiar. He was seated at his desk and didn't seem to mind letting us all stand. Kellyann and J.J. stood further away. Kellyann looked uncomfortable and shaken. She wasn't wearing her lunch anymore, but she was a mess, with red spots on her blouse and skirt and sticky cheese in her hair.

Lalo was standing next to me. He looked amazingly calm and relaxed, like he knew exactly why he was there.

Mrs. Gonzalez had already given her view of the events in the cafeteria. Once again, it didn't make me look very good. I was sure I was in trouble again. Maybe this was Strike Three. Maybe the baseball game was over for me. But somehow I didn't care. This time it felt much better.

After hearing Mrs. Gonzalez's account, Mr. Barnes got up, walked around his desk and stood between the four of us. He had his arms crossed and was holding his funky reading glasses in one hand. He looked at Kellyann and J.J., then at

Lalo and finally at me. He kept looking at me. He seemed tired. Then he turned again to Kellyann.

"Miss Moore, what's your side of the story?" he asked.

Kellyann started slowly. She was choosing her words
5 carefully. She painted a picture of herself and J.J. as unfortunate victims who hadn't been doing anything wrong. I had interrupted their lunch and unfairly accused them of doing something they would *never* do in a million years. She looked upset, like her feelings had been hurt. She was a good actor.
10 J.J. nodded the whole time, like he would have told it exactly the same way.

Mr. Barnes nodded too. He turned back to me.

"Why do I get the feeling she's telling the truth, Miss Quinn?" he said.

15 "Because you don't know the full story, Mr. Barnes," I said. Lalo looked over at me.

Mr. Barnes lifted his tired eyebrow. "Tell me then. What part of the story am I missing?"

"The part about my locker. You see, it doesn't work. Any-
20 one can open it," I said. "It's been like that for weeks. Only three people know about it: Jason Lee and these two."

I didn't feel like using their names. They glared at me.

"So what are you saying, Miss Quinn?" he asked.

"One of them could have taken my gym bag out of my
25 locker and put the spray cans in it, so that it looked like I had painted the graffiti," I said. "It had to be someone with racist views. Someone who wasn't happy with me. Like Kellyann. On Friday I disagreed with her view of black activism and told her I didn't want to go bowling with her."

30 Kellyann's mouth dropped open. "That's *so* not true!"

Mr. Barnes watched her reaction, then turned back to me. "What about Jason Lee? He could have also done it."

Lalo frowned and shook his head.

"Jason? No way. He had no reason," I said. "Anyway, these guys have already admitted it. That's what the scene in the cafeteria was all about."

"I didn't admit anything!" Kellyann squealed.

"Me neither!" J.J. said.

"Lalo Mendez is my witness," I said.

Mr. Barnes looked at Lalo. "Is that true, Mr. Mendez?"

Lalo nodded.

"That's a lie!" J.J. said. "I was there. Kellyann didn't say anything like that."

"J.J. didn't either," Kellyann said. "I'm his witness."

They looked at each other and at Mr. Barnes confidently. Mr. Barnes rubbed his eyes and sighed.

"It sounds like it's your word against theirs, Miss Quinn," he said.

Lalo cleared his throat and spoke for the first time.

"Not exactly," he said.

He reached into the pocket of his bomber jacket and pulled out his cell phone. He held it up and tapped the screen. A recording started. There was cafeteria noise and the sound of voices, including my own. We heard the whole conversation. Mr. Barnes listened, both of his eyebrows slowly rising. Kellyann's face was frozen. J.J. stared at the floor. We heard the insults and finally the crash of Kellyann's lunch tray. Lalo stopped the recording. The room was silent. Mr. Barnes rubbed his eyes again. Kellyann looked like she wanted to wrap her pretty fingers around Lalo's neck. Finally Mr. Barnes spoke.

"Miss Quinn, Mr. Mendez, you can go now," he said.

We debated as we walked down the hallway.
"She hates me more than she hates you," Lalo said.
"No, she definitely hates me more," I said.
5   "No way," he said. "You saw that look she gave me."
It felt like our friendship had just moved to a whole new level. I wanted to enjoy that feeling.
Were Kellyann and J.J. going to try to get revenge? Probably. Did I care? At that moment, not one bit.

Chapter 15

Mae was watching and waiting.

"Well? Come on! What do you think?" she said.

I swirled the juice around a little longer in my mouth. Then I swallowed.

"Awesome," I said. "I've never tasted cider like this." 5

It was the honest-to-god truth. Fresh, home-made apple cider was a new experience for me. Mae told me she made it every year – and this year from the apples we'd picked together. That made the taste even more special.

"I told you," she said. "Fresh is the best. I've got a big bottle 10 ready for you to take home."

The afternoon light was fading. We'd finished raking up the fallen leaves and putting them into her compost. I stared at the half-empty glass of cider.

"Matty loved this stuff. Apple was his favorite," I said. 15

Mae looked at me. "I've been thinking about you, Iris Quinn – why y'all moved away from Weed," she said. "I get it. Sometimes you have to leave a place to put the past behind you. Ain't that right?"

"That's what Mom thinks. But you don't really leave it, or 20 it doesn't leave you. So what's the point?" I said.

"That's true too," she said, her voice trailing off.

We were both speaking from experience, but she had a lot more of it. I began to wonder.

"Why did you leave Georgia?" I asked. 25

Mae looked at me. Her eyes wandered up to the yellowing leaves on the trees. She sighed.

"It was the early 60s. The world was a whole lot different then. Macon, Georgia was different. I was 23 and I had a decent job in a ticket office. I was still living at home with my mama, but I was independent. My best friend, Glenda, was studying at a university in Atlanta. She was really smart. It was hard enough for black folks to get into a university, but for a black woman it was even harder. But she did it. I was so proud of her. But there was a lot happening at that time."

"You mean the civil rights movement?" I asked.

"You've been doing your homework," she said. "Yeah, white folks weren't making life easy for us, that's for sure. Black folks got treated badly. But we pushed back, and we had Dr. King. He gave us hope.

Glenda joined a student group that was peacefully protesting on buses and in bus stations. They had been in the news a lot."

I couldn't believe what I was hearing. "Wait. Do you mean the Freedom Rides?" I said.

"That was what they called them, yes," she said. "There was violence going on and people were getting hurt. It was terrible. I didn't want Glenda to do it – I was really scared. But that girl had a hard head. She wouldn't listen, and I couldn't let her go alone. So I went with her."

"Are you telling me you were a *Freedom Rider*?" I said, stunned. It was like all the stuff from Social Studies was coming to life in front of my eyes.

"I didn't want her to get hurt," she said. "We got on a bus in Atlanta going to Montgomery, Alabama. I'll never forget it. My first time outside the state of Georgia. Angry white people were screaming and shouting when we got on the bus. But the worst was when we got to Montgomery."

I already knew what she was going to say.

"When we got off the bus, they beat us. Those white men beat us badly. Someone punched me. Glenda got hit on the head with a stick. She was bleeding and couldn't stand up. I stayed with her until the police took us to jail."

I thought about the mugshots that Lalo had shown us and the girl in one photo who I felt like I knew.

"Did the police take your photo?" I asked.

"Oh yes," she said. "That's what got me in trouble back in Macon. People saw my photo in the newspapers. I lost my job, people said terrible things to me in the streets, and my mama got scary phone calls. It was too much. So finally I left. I didn't want my mama to suffer."

I tried to imagine a young Mae and how it must have felt, everything she went through, but I couldn't.

"Do you regret it? I mean, the bus ride?" I asked.

Mae thought for a moment. "If Glenda hadn't gone, I never would have. I was there because of her. It was right, what we did. I'm proud of that. But I was no hero."

"Yes, you were. You were a friend," I said.

Mae was quiet. She looked at the ground.

"She meant a lot to me," she said.

Walking home, I thought about Mae's amazing story. She had been part of history. If only I had known before our presentation! Mae's words about being there for her friend were still in my ears. I thought of Lalo in the school cafeteria and in Mr. Barnes's office.

The air was getting cooler as the sun disappeared behind the shoebox houses on Vine Street. My thoughts wandered. I saw how Hartford was a meeting place. I'd met Mae, then Lalo. We'd come from different places but shared things in
5 common. I thought about Angel and Kellyann too. Not all meetings were nice, but they all meant something, even if I didn't understand exactly what. I still felt empty inside. I missed Weed and thought about my life there every day. But something had changed. Hartford had a meaning that it
10 hadn't had before.

I could hear the sounds of the city in the early evening breeze. A siren grew louder. I turned and saw, two blocks away, a police car racing past on Franklin with its blue lights flashing. Those lights were taking on a different meaning too.
15 Another siren came from somewhere else, moving fast in the same direction. I could hear screeching tires. It sounded like the corner of Sutter and Franklin. The two police cars were speeding towards Bryant Park.

Bryant Park, I thought. Coming home on the school bus,
20 Lalo had said he wanted to go there. Tyrell and some other boys were meeting for a game. When he'd mentioned Tyrell, I'd given him a tiny smile and he'd smiled back. I stopped, took out my phone and rang him. After the fourth ring, I knew Lalo wasn't going to answer. Maybe he was playing
25 basketball … or maybe something was wrong. My heart started beating hard.

It was like I was running before I even knew I was running. I ran back past Mae's house and, without stopping, tossed my backpack over the fence and into her garden. I
30 turned left at the corner and ran up Bentley to Sutter, then right along Sutter towards Franklin. I was going to be late for

dinner, but this was too important. When I reached Franklin, my legs were heavy and I was breathing so hard my chest hurt. I had to stop for the traffic light, but when it quickly turned green, I shot across the street. Jason was cleaning the sidewalk in front of the grocery store. Seeing me running 5 like that towards the park, he knew something was wrong. He dropped what he was doing and ran after me. When we reached the park, I almost couldn't stand up. The courts, grass, benches, trees and nearby houses were all dancing in blue flashing light. There was a small crowd of people. 10

As we neared the courts, I saw someone on the ground. *Lalo?* My heart was pumping. We pushed past the people. A boy was lying on his stomach. His T-shirt was torn and there was blood on his shirt, head and face. His teeth were bright in the dim light, but he wasn't smiling. A policeman 15 was kneeling on his back, pulling his arms behind him.

"Oh God," I said. It was Tyrell.

Tyrell was trying to look up at something. I followed his eyes to a second cop who was wrestling with someone. Again I thought of Lalo, but the person was too small. It was 20 a boy, and he was screaming as he shook himself free from the cop, his arms swinging wildly. It was Dion. The cop was the same tough-looking dude that had given Tyrell a hard time the week before.

I could see terror in Dion's eyes and face. He was in 25 another world, out of control, caught in one of his episodes that Lalo had described to me and that I knew all too well from Matty. Seeing Dion, an electric charge shot through me – an impulse to act. Matty had needed someone there with him. Dion did too. 30

In a panic, Dion pushed the cop away and the man lost his balance and nearly fell. He found his feet again and angrily pulled something out of his belt and pointed it at Dion. It was pepper spray. Dion, caught between a concrete wall and
5 a bike stand, had nowhere to go. Like a cornered tiger, he flipped out and ran at the cop, screaming. The pepper spray can flew out of the cop's hand and tumbled across the court. That was when the cop reached for his service revolver ...

It's a confusion of sounds, images, sensations – Jason yelling,
10 *"Iris, no!" – Mom calling to me, "Have you seen Matty?" – an angry man's voice saying, "Are you crazy?" – distant voices yelling and screaming, mixing with the swirl of flashing lights – fire truck red, police car blue – the crackle of a two-way radio – a mangled bike – my tired legs somehow covering one more time-*
15 *less distance – and a revolver pointed straight at me.*

I'm looking into the hard eyes of a cop with a gun. I see the sweat on his face. What's going through his head? Is he going to squeeze the trigger? How did I get here? I'm between him and Dion, my hands raised in front of me.
20 *"Stop. Don't," I hear myself say. Tears are streaming down my cheeks.*

"GET OUT OF THE WAY!" he yells.

I hear myself again. "He's just freaked out. I can calm him down. He doesn't mean any harm. Please." I'm trying any words
25 *that will make him put his gun away.*

The expressions on his face change from surprised to angry to nervous to puzzled. I keep my hands in front of me where he can see them. I turn to Dion. His eyes are wild, he's breathing heavily, his whole body is shaking, he can't stand still, he doesn't know where to look or turn. I wait for him to recognize me, to meet my eyes.

"Hey, Dion. It's okay," I say.

I look back at the cop, his gun pointed at Dion again, like he's ready to shoot. "Please," I say to him again, waiting for him 5
to see me, then I turn back to Dion.

"Dion, look at me. You're upset, I know. I understand. Just don't run. Please stay here." I point to the ground. I'm trying to be calm. He looks like he's going to run and I'm praying that he won't. Slowly I squat down close to the ground, like I used to do 10
with Matty. "Come on, Dion." I carefully sit down cross-legged, my hands still in the air. "Let's be upset, right here, you and me." His eyes are moving between me and the cop with the gun. "Look at me, Dion. Never mind him. I'm here. Iris, remember?"

"Iris," he says with a dry throat. He starts to sit down. 15

"Slowly," I say, looking straight into his wild eyes.

He plops down hard on his butt. He's still shaking and breathing hard. The tears come and we're both crying. Our foreheads touch. I stroke his arms and shoulders.

"Let's get him out of here," the cop said behind me. 20

I turned my head and saw he was talking to the other cop. His revolver was back in his belt. Tyrell was still on his stomach, his wrists behind him in handcuffs. They pulled him to his feet.

"I didn't do *nothin'*, man," Tyrell complained. 25

They walked him to a squad car. People were shouting at the police, protesting, filming them with their smartphones. Above the noise I heard another voice.

"Dion!" It was a woman and she sounded desperate. "Let me get through! That's my boy!" she cried. A moment later she was kneeling next to us.

"Dion, my God, child, what happened? Are you okay?" she said. She looked at him, then at me.

He threw his arms around her. "Mama," he said.

Angel was standing behind her. She looked as worried as her mom did. Our eyes met.

"They didn't do anything, Mama," Dion said.

"Who didn't, sweetheart?" she asked.

"Tyrell and Lalo. They were just playing ball," he said.

"Lalo?" I said. I stood up and looked over at the squad cars. The cops were putting Tyrell into the back seat of one of them. Someone was already in there. I ran to the car.

"You've got a lot of nerve, little girl," someone said. I turned and it was the tough-guy cop who had held the gun. "I should arrest your ass."

"I'm not your little girl," I said. "And I should report your ass."

He stepped towards me, then his partner called to him.

"Duncan! Let's go!"

He sneered at me and got into the police car. Through the side window I could see Lalo in the back seat. Like Tyrell, he was in handcuffs. His hair was messed up and he had a bruise on the side of his face. He turned his head and saw me. His eyes seemed to sparkle and a thin smile spread over his quiet face. Then the police car drove away.

Chapter 16

I had never seen Mom and Dad look like that before. The shock on their faces when they saw their daughter on the evening news, facing a cop with a gun. The scene looked totally crazy. It was hard to believe that was really me.

"My God, Iris, what were you thinking?! You could have been killed!" Mom said. Dad leaned forward in his chair and put his head in his hands.

The day after the 'Bryant Park police incident', as the news reporter called it, I still hadn't told my parents everything that had happened. I'd just said that some kids had been arrested – nothing about Dion and the hot-headed cop. I didn't want to freak them out. But I wasn't expecting the whole thing to be on the evening news.

It had been a weird school day. Nobody had said anything to me about the park, but the way people were looking at me, I could see that it was on their minds. Lalo and Tyrell weren't at school, and everyone knew why. My teachers had been careful not to give me too much work, like I was a hospital patient or something. On the way home, there were no jokes or lighthearted comments from Chance the bus driver. At my stop, he had quietly watched me get off the bus and said, "Take it easy, Iris."

I'm pretty sure most people didn't understand what had happened and why I'd done what I'd done. How could they know what was going on in my head? But after we watched it on the news, I wanted Mom and Dad to know.

"I had no choice. I had to do it," I said.

"What are you talking about?" Dad answered.

A wave of emotion hit me and the tears and snot flowed again.

5 "I wasn't there when Matty needed me. This time I *was* there. I *had to* do something. Dion *needed* me," I said.

Mom's mouth dropped open.

"Oh no, no, no, Iris!" she said quietly, grabbing my shoulders and searching my face like she'd lost something. "Please 10 tell me you don't really believe that you–"

Dad stepped forward.

"Iris. The way you protected Dion was ... beautiful. Hard to watch, but beautiful. But what happened to Matty was nobody's fault. Nobody could protect him from himself. Or 15 from life."

"Yes, we had to!" I cried.

"We loved him and we did all we could," Mom said. A tear slid down her cheek.

I thought about what they were saying. Part of me didn't 20 want to believe it. Mom and Dad looked at each other for a long time, like maybe they didn't believe it themselves. Or maybe they were just realizing it.

An image came into my head. I saw myself taking a long jump shot in slow motion. I held the basketball, this perfect 25 round orb, in my hands and, as I let it go, the ball floated through the air in a long, beautiful arc, spinning magically, freely. It belonged to no one and where it would land was anybody's guess.

I was tidying up the kitchen after dinner when a text came.

"Hola chica. I'm home. All is good."

I dropped what I was doing, ran upstairs to my room and rang Lalo. I wanted to know everything.

"It wasn't so bad," he said. "Some of the cops at the police station even told me they were sorry. They were nice. Not like hard-ass Officer Duncan."

"That's the guy, right?" I asked.

"Yeah, I got his badge number too," he said.

He told me how the two officers had arrived at the basketball courts and started shooting baskets with them. Everything seemed cool. Then Officer Duncan had wanted to search Tyrell. Again.

"Tyrell said no this time. So the dude got rough with him – like really rough. It hurt to watch, but I filmed it on my phone. When Duncan saw that, he came after me."

"I saw the bruise on your face."

"Yeah, he roughed me up, threw me to the ground."

"And your phone?"

"I handed it to some kids and one of them disappeared with it. My mom had it when I came home."

"Wow. You have to do something with that, Lalo."

"I already did. I uploaded the film and sent it to the Hartford Journal and to Channel 3 News."

"*Yes!* Nice move."

"Everybody's going to know who that dude is."

"Did they take a mugshot of you at the police station?"

"Yeah, that was weird. I thought of all those Freedom Riders, Iris. I could feel them."

"When this is all over, there's somebody who I'd like you to meet."

"Yeah? ... I saw what you did out there, Iris. You are one crazy girl. *Una chica loca*."

"And you are one *chico loco*."

"Yeah, well ... just fighting for our rights."

5 "I don't know what I'm fighting for ... but I know who my friends are."

One of the last things Lalo told me was that Tyrell had called him and thanked him. I could hear in his voice how much that meant to him. Tyrell had also promised to help
10 him with his jump shot. Lalo and basketball still didn't fit together for me.

"Is that what you want?" I asked. There was a pause.

"I think you know what I want. But for now I'll take what I can get," he said.

15 I could hear him smiling.

Chapter 17

The next day I was cleaning my room when I heard the door-bell and then Mom's voice at the front door.

"Iris? Yes, sure, come on in." Then her voice got louder. "IRIS! You have visitors!"

Visitors? Plural? I wasn't even expecting one visitor.   5

They were standing in the hallway as I came down the stairs. I was so surprised, I stopped halfway down.

"Don't just stand there, come on down!" Mom said.

Dion was smiling from ear to ear. Angel, behind him, had an uneasy, almost embarrassed look on her face.   10

"Hi, Iris!" Dion said loudly.

"Dion ...," I said.

Angel said something softly, then cleared her throat and spoke louder. "Dion wanted to come and see you. Our mom found out your address."   15

I was speechless. Mom looked at me impatiently.

"Erm, ... and now you're here," I said.

Dad came in from the living room. He recognized Dion from the TV news.

"Oh, hello," he said. "What a nice surprise!"   20

Dion and Angel smiled. Dion looked around, checking out the place. He pointed to the wall next to him.

"There's a hole in the wall," he said.

"Dion!" Angel said, slapping his finger.

Mom smiled at Dion. "You noticed that," she said.   25

We both looked at Dad, who scratched his head.

"Yeah," he said. "We need to fix that."

"Well, can I take your jackets?" Mom said. "We're so glad you're here. Right, Iris?"

I was still stunned. "Erm, yeah, sure!"

5 We moved to the kitchen and sat down at the table. Mom brought out milk and oatmeal cookies.

"I can make hot cocoa, if anyone would like some," she said. Angel looked uncomfortable.

"Oh no, thank you, this is fine," she said. Dion already had 10 a cookie in his mouth.

Mom led the conversation with lots of questions. It was more than a little strange when Angel and I had to explain which classes we had together. It was only then that Mom realized who Angel was.

15 "Oh, you're *Angel Mitchell!* Of course!" she said.

She had no idea how awkward that was for me. I shifted in my chair and rolled my eyes at her.

Dad stood by the sink, looking amused.

Mom was mostly interested in Dion. Soon they were 20 chatting and he told her all about his day and everything he liked and didn't like. He said he didn't like police.

"I can understand that," she said. "But, you know, they're not all bad. Iris's uncle is a policeman. He's a good guy."

"Mom, please," I protested. I don't know why that embar- 25 rassed me, but it did. She ignored me.

"I'm sorry about what happened in the park," she told Dion. "That was just awful."

Dion nodded. His face was blank, like he had already packed that memory away somewhere. He took another 30 cookie.

"Iris was very brave, wasn't she?" Mom said.

"Yeah," Dion said.

I couldn't listen. "Oh, stop," I said. "It wasn't brave."

Angel looked straight at me. "What was it then?"

I thought for a second. "That cop knew I was white."

Angel was quiet. Then she said, "Anyway, it doesn't matter ₅ anymore. Right?"

"It doesn't ... but it does," I said to her.

We looked at each other. She nodded. "Yeah, it does."

We were standing at the front door and Angel and Dion were putting their jackets on. ₁₀

"Come back and see us again, guys. It was really nice to meet you," Mom said.

"It was nice to meet you too," Angel said. She looked relieved. "Thank you for the cookies. Right, Dion?"

"Yeah," he said, smiling and looking at his feet. ₁₅

I tried to give him a fist bump and instead he hugged me. It felt great and awkward at the same time.

"I almost forgot," Angel said, looking at me. "My mom says hello. And thank you," she said.

I didn't know what to say. ₂₀

"When are you going to come to the park?" Dion asked.

"I don't know, Dion. Sometime soon, I'm sure," I said.

"Well, we're walking over there now," Angel said.

She waited for me to take up the invitation.

I never dreamed I would ever walk down Vine Street together ₂₅ with Angel or Dion. It was another one of those weird things. Dion was trying to dribble my basketball as we walked. Angel and I debated our strengths on the court. It was amazing that we were actually talking and having a normal conversation, but it was still early in the game.

"Your jump shot is pretty good," she said. "Almost as good as mine."

5 "Almost as good? Oh, please," I said. "You know, I could show you a few things about dribbling."

"Hm," she said. "Maybe, maybe not."

We walked past Mae's house and I could see her standing in the garden with the garden hose in her hand. She was
10 spraying water around, the way she had shown me. She heard our voices and looked up.

"Well, well," she said, shaking her head and smiling. "That is a sight I was not expecting today."

We stopped and said hello. I realized Angel was not a
15 stranger to her.

"Wait. You–?" I said to Mae, pointing at Angel.

"Hi, Mae!" Dion interrupted. "We're going to play basketball!"

"Your mama told me about you, Dion," she said. "It looks
20 like you're okay, thank the Lord."

Angel saw that I was confused.

"Mae is a family friend. She knows our granny," she said. "But how do *you* know her?"

"What do you mean? We're neighbors!" I said.

25 "Iris Quinn does most of the work in this garden," Mae chuckled.

"That's what it feels like," I said.

I couldn't believe how weird this all was.

"So you knew the whole time, Mae. Why didn't you want
30 to tell me?" I asked.

Angel seemed as interested as I was.

"Tell you what?" Mae said. "I didn't want to get in the way. I knew you two were going to work out your problems sooner or later."

Angel and I looked at each other, amazed.

"Can I do that?" Dion said, pointing at Mae's garden hose. 5

"Of course you can. Come on in here, child!" Mae said.

Dion opened the gate and went into the garden. She handed him the hose.

"Be sure you don't just water in one place," Mae said.

He tried to spray the water around like Mae had, but he 10 did it too hard and the water splattered all over us.

"Hey!" I yelled.

Angel jumped back. "Dion, you little–!"

Mae and Dion laughed.

"I think Dion knows what he's doin'," she said. "Smart boy, 15 Dion," she said, patting him on the shoulder.

Angel wiped her face and looked at me. "Are you thinking what I'm thinking?"

I looked at Dion and back at her. "There's one of him and two of us," I said. 20

"Let's get him," she said.

Dion's eyes got big and he squealed with delight.

Vocabulary

Abbreviations
sb. = somebody; sth. = something;
etw. = etwas; jmdn. = jemanden; jmdm. = jemandem;
umg. = umgangssprachlich

A
aisle [aɪl] Gang
anger [ˈæŋɡə] Ärger
(to) **annoy** [əˈnɔɪ] nerven
  annoying nervig
(to) **announce** sth. [əˈnaʊns] etw.
  ankündigen
apparently [əˈpærəntli]
  anscheinend
approval [əˈpruːvl] Zustimmung
apron [ˈeɪprən] Schürze
attitude [ˈætɪtjuːd] Haltung,
  Einstellung
(to) **avoid** sth. [əˈvɔɪd] etw.
  vermeiden
awkward [ˈɔːkwəd] unan-
  genehm

B
badass [ˈbædæs] *umg.* super;
  krass
barely [ˈbeərli] kaum
bead [biːd] Perle
belt [belt] Gürtel
bench [bentʃ] Bank

big-mouthed [ˈbɪɡ maʊðd]
  großmäulig
(to) **blurt** sth. **out** [blɜːt] mit etw.
  herausplatzen
(to) **bother** sb. [ˈbɒðə] jmdn.
  stören
  (to) **feel hot and**
  bothered wütend sein
(to) **braid** sth. [breɪd] etw.
  flechten
branch [brɑːntʃ] Ast, Zweig
bright [braɪt] bunt
(to) **brighten** up sth. [ˈbraɪtn]
  etw. aufhellen
(to) **bounce** [baʊns] hüpfen,
  springen
bucket [ˈbʌkɪt] Eimer
butt [bʌt] Po, Hintern
button-down [ˈbʌtn daʊn]:
  button-down shirt *Hemd*
  mit fest geknöpftem Kragen

C
chest [tʃest] Brust
(to) **chuckle** [ˈtʃʌkl] kichern

(to) **clap** [klæp]: (to) **clap one's hands** in die Hände klatschen

clapboard house ['klæbɔːd haʊs] Schindelhaus

(to) **click** [klɪk]: (to) **click one's tongue** mit der Zunge schnalzen

cocky ['kɒki] anmaßend, eingebildet

concrete ['kɒŋkriːt] Beton

county courthouse ['kaʊnti 'kɔːthaʊs] Bezirksgericht

crack [kræk] Riss

(to) **crackle** ['krækl] knacken, knistern

crap [kræp] *umg.* Mist

crappy [kræpi] *umg.* beschissen

curious ['kjʊəriəs] interessant; interessiert

D

dang [dæŋ] *umg.* verdammt

daze [deɪz]: (to) **be in a daze** ganz benommen sein

(to) **depend** on sth. [dɪ'pend] von etw. abhängen

(to) **deserve** sth. [dɪ'zɜːv] etw. verdienen

(to) **develop** sth. [dɪ'veləp] etw. entwickeln

distraction [dɪ'strækʃn] Ablenkung

dome [dəʊm] Kuppeldach

dope [dəʊp] *umg.* super, cool

drawer [drɔː] Schublade

drill [drɪl] Bohrer

dude [duːd] Typ; *umg.* Alter

dust [dʌst] Staub

E

eager ['iːgə] begierig

either ['aɪðə] auch
  either ... or entweder ... oder

(to) **exhale** [eks'heɪl] ausatmen

eyebrow ['aɪbraʊ] Augenbraue

F

faded [feɪdɪd] verblichen, verwaschen

file [faɪl] Akte

fist bump ['fɪst bʌmp] *Abklatschen mit der Faust*

(to) **flip** sth. [flɪp]: (to) **flip a switch** einen Schalter umlegen

(to) **frisk** sb. [frɪsk] jmd. abtasten

folder ['fəʊldə] Mappe, Ordner

folks [fəʊks] Leute

foreign ['fɒrən] fremd, ausländisch

fork [fɔːrk] Gabel

(to) **freak** sb. out [friːk] jmdn. in Angst versetzen

(to) **frown** [fraʊn] die Stirn runzeln

funky ['fʌŋki] abgefahren, ungewöhnlich

G

geez [dʒiːs] *umg.* du meine Güte

gentle ['dʒentl] sanft

(to) **giggle** ['gɪgl] kichern

goodness [ˈɡʊdnəs]: **my goodness**   du liebe Güte
gross [ɡrəʊs]   eklig
guy [ɡaɪ]   Typ

H
(to) **handle** sth. [ˈhændl]   etw.
bewältigen, mit etw. umgehen
hard-nosed [ˌhɑːd ˈnəʊzd]
unnachgiebig
hell [hel]: **what the hell**   was
zum Teufel
high-top [ˈhaɪ tɒp]: **high-top
sneakers**   *Turnschuhe, die bis
über die Knöchel gehen*
hip [hɪp]   Hüfte
hook [hʊk]   Haken
hose [həʊz]: **garden hose**   Gar-
tenschlauch
hot-headed [ˌhɒt ˈhedɪd]   hitz-
köpfig

I
immaculate [ɪˈmækjələt]   makel-
los
(to) **injure** sb./sth. [ˈɪndʒə]
jmdn./etw. verletzten
interrogation [ɪnˌterəˈɡeɪʃn]
Verhör
(to) **insist** on sth. [ɪnˈsɪst]   auf
etw. bestehen

J
jerk [dʒɜːk]   Trottel
jock [dʒɒk]   Sportler(in);
Sportfanatiker(in)

(to) **judge** sb./sth. [dʒʌdʒ]   jmdn./
etw. bewerten

K
knuckle [ˈnʌkl]   (Finger-)Knöchel

L
lame [leɪm]   *umg.* schwach, lahm;
langweilig
librarian [laɪˈbreəriən]   Bibliothe-
kar(in)
lippy [ˈlɪpi]   *umg.* frech
lock [lɒk]   Schloss (*Tür*)
(to) **lock** sth.   etw. abschließen
(to) **lock eyes**   Augen/Blicke
treffen sich
(to) **loot** sth. [luːt]   etw. aus-
plündern

M
(to) **moan** [məʊn]   stöhnen
mugshot [ˈmʌɡʃɒt]   *umg.* Fahn-
dungsfoto

N
nasty [ˈnɑːsti]   schlimm
neat [niːt]   ordentlich
newbie [ˈnjuːbi]   Neuling
nightstick [ˈnaɪtstɪk]   Schlag-
stock

O
obviously [ˈɒbviəsli]   offen-
sichtlich
opponent [əˈpəʊnənt]   Geg-
ner(in)

P

party pooper [ˈpɑːrti puːpə] *umg.*
Spielverderber(in)

patrol car [pəˈtrəʊl kɑː] Strei-
fenwagen

peeling [piːlɪŋ] *hier*: sich
ablösend

permission [pəˈmɪʃn] Erlaubnis

pig-headed [ˌpɪg ˈhedɪd] stur

pissed-off [pɪst ɒf] *umg.*
(stink-)sauer

pistol [ˈpɪstl] Pistole
(to) **be hotter than a
pistol** *Sport:* sehr gut drauf
sein, sehr gut spielen

posture [ˈpɒstʃə] Köperhaltung

prickly [ˈprɪkli] leicht reizbar,
aufbrausend

(to) **puke** [pjuːk] sich erbrechen

pushback [ˈpʊʃbæk] Widerstand

pushy [ˈpʊʃi] penetrant, aggres-
siv

puzzled [ˈpʌzld] verständnislos,
verwirrt

R

racial [ˈreɪʃl] rassistisch

(to) **recognize** sth. [ˈrekəgnaɪz]
etw. (wieder-)erkennen

referee [ˌrefəˈriː] Schieds-
richter(in)

(to) **refuse** sth. [rɪˈfjuːz] etw.
verweigern

regret [rɪˈgret] Bedauern

ribbon [ˈrɪbən] Schleife

ridiculous [rɪˈdɪkjələs] lächerlich

riot [ˈraɪət] Unruhen, Ausschrei-
tungen

(to) **rip** sth. [rɪp] reißen; heraus-
reißen

rotten [ˈrɒtn] verfault

rough [rʌf] rau, hart
(to) **rough** sb. up grob zu
jmdm. werden; jmdn. zusam-
menschlagen

rumble [ˈrʌmbl] Grollen, Knurren

S

sacred [ˈseɪkrɪd] heilig

separate [ˈseprət] getrennt

siblings [ˈsɪblɪŋs] Geschwister

sit-in [ˈsɪt ɪn] Sitzstreik

(to) **shift** [ʃɪft]: (to) **shift in one's
seat** auf dem Stuhl herum-
rutschen

(to) **shovel** sth. [ˈʃʌvl] etw.
schaufeln

(to) **shrug** [ʃrʌg] die Achseln
zucken

(to) **shuffle** [ˈʃʌfl] schlurfen

(to) **slap** sth. [slæp] etw. schlagen

slob [slɒb] *Person, die unordent-
lich und faul ist*

(to) **slump** [slʌmp] fallen

smooth [smuːð] glatt
smooth-talking wortge-
wandt

(to) **snatch** sth. [snætʃ] sich etw.
schnappen; nach etw. greifen

snot [snɒt] *umg.* Rotz

snow-capped [snəʊ kæpd] mit
Schnee bedeckt

soft [sɒft] weich

speechless ['spiːtʃləs]   sprachlos
spice [spaɪs]   Gewürz
(to) **steam** [stiːm]   dampfen;
  wütend sein
stuffed animal [ˌstʌft
  'ænɪml]   *hier:* Kuscheltier
(to) **suck** [sʌk]   ätzend sein
  sucky   blöd, nervig
(to) **swear** [sweə]   schwören
(to) **sweep** [swiːp]   fegen

T
tangle ['tæŋgl]   Knäuel, Gewirr
tasteless ['teɪstləs]   geschmack-
  los
tasty ['teɪsti]   lecker
thick [θɪk]**: thick air**   dicke Luft
thrilled [θrɪld]**:** (to) **be**
  thrilled   außer sich sein vor
  Freude
throat [θrəʊt]**:** (to) **clear one's**
  throat   sich räuspern
touchy ['tʌtʃi]   heikel, empfindlich
tough-looking [tʌf lʊkɪŋ]   hart/
  unnachgiebig aussehend
tray [treɪ]   Tablett
trigger ['trɪgə]   Abzug
troublemaker ['trʌblmeɪkə]
  Unruhestifter(in)

two-way radio
  [ˌtuː weɪ 'reɪdiəʊ]   Funk-
  sprechgerät

U
ugly ['ʌgli]   hässlich
upset [ˌʌp'set]   aufgeregt, sauer

W
wall mural [wɔːl 'mjʊərəl]   Wand-
  gemälde
weird [wɪəd]   seltsam
whatever [wɒt'evə]   was auch
  immer
wind-chimes ['wɪnd tʃaɪmz]
  Windspiele
wing [wɪŋ]   Flügel
witness ['wɪtnəs]   Zeuge(-in)
(to) **wrap sb./sth.** [ræp]   jmdn./
  etw. umarmen
wrinkle ['rɪŋkl]   Falte

Y
(to) **yell** [jel]   schreien

Z
zillion ['zɪljən]   *umg.* zigtausend